# In All Humility
*Saying No to Last Generation Theology*

# In All Humility

*Saying No to Last Generation Theology*

Reinder Bruinsma

**Oak & Acorn**
PUBLISHING
Westlake Village, California

*In All Humility* Copyright © 2018 by Reinder Bruinsma

All rights reserved. Printed in the United States of America. No part of this book may be used or reproduced in any manner whatsoever without written permission except in the case of brief quotations embodied in critical articles or reviews. Unless otherwise indicated, all Scripture quotations are from the New International Version of the Bible, © 2011, by Broadman and Holman Publishers (Nashville, TN). Used by permission.

Texts credited to the New Living Translation are from the Holy Bible, New Living Translation, copyright © 2015. Used by permission of the Tyndale House Publishers, Inc., Wheaton, IL. All rights reserved.

For information contact:
Oak & Acorn Publishing
PO Box 5005
Westlake Village, CA 91359-5005

Cover image: iStock
Cover design by Natalie Falk and Oak & Acorn Publishing

First Edition 2018

10 9 8 7 6 5 4 3 2 1

# Contents

Foreword .................................................. ix

Preface .................................................. xiii

Chapter 1
An Exercise in Humility ..................................... 1

Chapter 2
Last Generation Theology:
What it is and Where it Came From ......................... 13

Chapter 3
What is Sin? .............................................. 27

APPENDIX:
Comments of Ellen G. White on Sin and Sinlessness .......... 47

Chapter 4
How Human was Christ? The Biblical Answer ................. 49

APPENDIX:
Comments of Ellen G. White on
Christ's Human Nature ..................................... 69

Chapter 5
Ellen White on the Human Nature of Jesus Christ ............ 73

Chapter 6
Perfection: Possible or Impossible? ........................ 91

APPENDIX:
Comments of Ellen G. White on Perfection .................. 117

Chapter 7
"Shaken" and on Our Own? .................................. 125

Chapter 8
Can We "Hasten" the Second Coming? ........................ 147

Chapter 9
In All Humility ........................................... 167

Bibliography .............................................. 173

# Foreword

There is an old expression that says, "May you live in interesting times!" The times in which Christianity—and particularly Seventh-day Adventism—exists today can certainly be called "interesting."

The theological situation in which we find ourselves is becoming increasingly diverse, polarized, and tense. Not that it has never been this way before; frequently throughout its relatively short history, Adventism has had intense theological divisions. But I wonder if they have been this severe, with at least the possibility of the future fracturing of the denomination.

Into this already "interesting" timeframe comes Dr. Reinder Bruinsma with a book that is both challenging and thoughtful: *In All Humility: Saying No to Last Generation Theology*—food for thought that every thinking Seventh-day Adventist should read.

This book is Bruinsma's examination and analysis of some of the recurring trends of thought in Adventism. As a former pastor, retired administrator and theologian, Bruinsma writes in a way that speaks to the heart of the current situation regarding Last Generation Theology.

Writing simply and clearly, without using theological jargon, he analyzes the current iteration of this issue. He shows how the idea started decades ago and has morphed into its present form, repeating the calls of former proponents proclaiming sinless perfection, asserting that the last generation before the second coming must have total victory over all sin, and making the claim that this will qualify them to live without an intercessor when Christ completes His ministry in the heavenly sanctuary.

Bruinsma points out that this logic wrongly puts humanity in control of when God facilitates the victorious return of Jesus to claim the righteous as His saints. This also leads to a pernicious form of judgmentalism—an "us versus them" attitude among the "perfected."

Another of the flawed ideas presented by Last Generation Theology proponents is that the vindication of God's character is dependent on human beings rising to the level of perfection and living perfectly.

A serious danger in "proving" this premise is the tendency of promoters to pick and choose among the Bible texts, failing to present all the texts pertinent to the subject, and ignoring the context in which they were written.

This trend also leads supporters of this theory to de-contextualize the writings of the most revered founder of the Seventh-day Adventist Church, Ellen G. White. And in the process, as Bruinsma documents, they ignore the sometimes paradoxical statements she made during her lengthy writing and teaching ministry. They, in essence, "cherry pick" those statements that support their ideology and ignore those that don't.

This is nothing new or exclusive—lots of people do this—but it is interesting that a group promoting perfection would use such an imperfect methodology to make the case for Last Generation Theology.

In the end, Bruinsma cautions Christians, and particularly Seventh-day Adventists, to humbly acknowledge that while we have beliefs informed by faith, we don't know everything about how the end of this world will come or when Jesus will return. Humility is essential to living faithfully in such circumstances.

This book is an opportunity for us to learn about the dangers of Last Generation Theology, to realize the importance of humbly accepting that we cannot know everything that is going to happen, and to reaffirm our faith that Jesus will never forsake us and is sufficient.

Ricardo Graham
President, Pacific Union Conference
August 2018

# Preface

This book is, as the subtitle tells you, about Last Generation Theology. Some of you may have heard these words, but I suspect many of you will wonder what this is all about. And maybe you are also wondering whether you are curious enough to read a whole book about it.

I have asked myself whether or not I should spend a considerable amount of my time writing about the topic of Last Generation Theology. Admittedly, I like writing; thus, from time to time, I look for a suitable subject for a new book. It must be a topic I believe I know something about, and it should be important and interesting enough that a sizable group of people would want to buy and read such a book. For a considerable amount of time I thought of writing a book about Last Generation Theology. I had come to the conclusion that the idea is gradually becoming ever more popular in certain Adventist circles, and I am convinced it will have an ever greater impact on the Adventist Church if it gains further support. In my opinion that impact is largely negative. That uneasy feeling gave me the desire to study the topic in more depth than I had done so far and to report my findings in a book.

*In All Humility: Saying No to Last Generation Theology* is the result. From the start I decided that I would try to write in the style of language that would make the book accessible to a broad readership. Although it is a rather complex subject, I have done my best to keep things as simple as possible. I hope I have succeeded and that what I have written will help many fellow believers in the Adventist Church to see what the issues are and to discern the deficiencies and dangers of Last Generation Theology. At the same time, I also hope that it will reinforce the faith of many readers in the assurance that Jesus Christ will come and that, if we are ready to meet Him, He will take us, imperfect though we are, with Him to our final destiny and make us forever perfect.

Zeewolde, the Netherlands
August 2018

# Chapter 1

# An Exercise In Humility

The proponents of Last Generation Theology are convinced that just before the end of this world there will be a last generation that has gained a complete victory over sin. This is when probation has closed and Christ has finished His work in His heavenly sanctuary. Those who are part of this last generation and have become perfect will now be able to live without a Mediator as they wait for the moment they will be changed "in the twinkling of an eye" (1 Corinthians 15:52) and will be taken by their Lord in their new, immortal bodies into their eternal heavenly abode.

This has some very important implications. How can human beings ever reach a state of perfect sinlessness? Believers in Last Generation Theology say this is possible. They point to Christ. He came to this world as one who was like us and, in spite of His humanness, was able to resist all sin. The kind of human nature He took upon Himself, we are told, was exactly like that of Adam *after* he had fallen into sin. And so, if Christ was in all respects like us, and could be sinless, it must also be possible for human beings to reach the state of sinlessness. This is a vital aspect of the "great controversy." The devil has argued that it is impossible for man to keep God's commandments. But the last generation proves it is, in fact, possible to be fully loyal to God. This vindicates God as a righteous God before the universe.

But there is more. Christ's return is directly connected with this: He cannot come until there is such a last generation of people who perfectly reflect His character. In later chapters I will refer in detail to the Bible texts and Ellen G. White statements on which this line of thinking rests. The fact that God's people will be reduced to a small remnant of perfect men and women further implies that there must be some kind of "shaking" in which it becomes clear who is going to make it during this short period before the curtain falls over human history.

Clearly there is quite a list of issues that we must look at. Here are the main questions we must try to answer:

- What kind of human nature did Christ take upon Himself when He became one of us?
- Is it possible for human beings to reach a state of perfection?
- How do we define sin?
- How do we define perfection?
- Is the existence of a perfect last generation an indispensable requirement for God's vindication before the universe?
- To what extent do we face the dangers of legalism and perfectionism as a result of Last Generation Theology?
- At some time before Christ's return, will there be a demarcation between those who will be saved and those who are already lost?
- What is the identity of the faithful remnant?
- Does the timing of the second coming depend on our human cooperation?

Each of these topics could be the subject for a separate book. I do not know whether I would be able to write such a series of book-length treatments. Even if I could, that is not what I want to do. I intend to limit myself to one small book, and, as I write, I will keep my eyes on the word-count feature of my word processing program! I hope that what I have to say is not just short and in non-technical language (so that people don't have to be trained theologians in order to follow my arguments), but that, at the same time, it will not be superficial. I will do my best, and I promise to be honest. When there are two sides to a coin, I will show both sides. I will not just quote the Bible texts that favor my point of view and search for statements in the writings of Ellen G. White that support my thinking. And when I do not know the answer to a particular question, I will not dodge that question or fabricate an answer that I cannot with full integrity accept myself.

**Limitations**

In dealing with the questions I have listed above we must keep one essential fact in mind. It is something we must always consider when embarking on a theological project. The word *theology* means "talk about God." And, let's be clear from the outset: God-talk is problematic. If it is true—as most Christians believe—that God is absolute and incomparable to human beings, who live (and speak and think) at a totally different (and infinitely lower) level, our God-talk will be deeply affected by the divine-human divide. Our speaking about God can always only be provisional. In formulating our doctrines we try to bring some structure in our (human) thinking about God, but it will always remain a fallible human attempt to express the inexpressible. Therefore, it must always remain a work in progress. Our theology is always subject to re-statement and revision. As soon as we have said something about God—about who He is and what He does—we must step back, bow our heads, and admit that what we have said falls far short of describing divine Reality, which goes far beyond our human concepts and conclusions.

This is an important point that we must underline as strongly as we can as we begin our journey into Last Generation Theology territory. Let us not be tempted to be too sure about things that we cannot be sure about. Yes, we believe that God has revealed Himself and the essence of His plan of salvation to us. He did so by giving us His Word—the Bible, this unique book that was written by people who were inspired by God, which means that during the writing process their thoughts were led by God's Holy Spirit. Realizing that human beings would need a further revelation, God sent His Son to this world. As we read in Hebrews 1:1-2: "In the past God spoke to our ancestors through the prophets at many times and in various ways, but now in these last days, he has spoken to us by his Son." Therefore, looking at Jesus we discover important things about God.

God's revelation may be limited, but it is sufficient for us. It tells us that God created us, that we owe Him our allegiance, and that He has made ample provision to save us from the mess we have caused by going our own ways. It carries the good news, that Christ came to live and die for us and that He will come again to take us to our eternal destiny.

God's revelation provides the knowledge we need in order to live as disciples of the Lord Jesus Christ and to be ready for the final events that will inaugurate God's kingdom in its full glory. But at the same time we must realize that many things will remain hidden from us. "The secret things belong to the Lord our God," but, on the other hand, "the things revealed belong to us and to our children" (Deuteronomy 29:29).

It is not difficult to make a list of things that are in the category of these "secret things." We know, for instance, that God created us, but He has left us in uncertainty about many aspects of this creative activity. We must be content with a concise story that tells us about our origin and about the responsibilities we have as created beings, but there are lots of blanks we cannot fill in. The Genesis record reveals that the first human beings made a wrong use of their free will, but God's Word remains silent about the question that has occupied so many minds ever since: How could evil emerge in a perfect universe?

We can have the assurance of salvation. "For God so loved the world that he gave his one and only Son, that whoever believes in him shall not perish but have eternal life" (John 3:16). Christ stated it very clearly, "Very truly I tell you, the one who believes has eternal life" (John 6:47). We believe that Jesus Christ has come to save us. He came to atone for our sins. We are redeemed by what Christ did for us. This assurance keeps us going, even when at times we are beset by doubt. The Bible uses various symbols and metaphors to describe this miracle of divine love. But do we have a clear picture of how exactly this atonement saves us? Couldn't God have chosen some other, much less painful, route? We may not agree with everything Zophar, one of Job's friends, said, but we can echo the questions he asked Job: "Can you solve the mysteries of God? Can you discover everything about the Almighty?" And we must conclude with Zophar that God's "knowledge is higher than the heavens" and is incomparable to anything else (Job 11:7-8, NLT).

The dilemma of human and animal suffering continues to baffle us. If God is love, why does He allow so many disasters and atrocities to happen? If He is almighty, He could presumably put a direct stop to all our misery. What could be the reason that He lets evil run its dramatic course? One answer—also given by Last Generation Theology defenders—is that it is all part of the great controversy between Christ and the power of evil, but that ultimately God will be vindicated. But how would that answer the eternal question of "why"? When all is said and done, we still fail to understand why God followed the strategy that He did.

The Bible contains much prophecy. Some (but only a part of it) predicts the future. Through the centuries many—together with large numbers of Seventh-day Adventists—have studied the Bible books of Daniel and Revelation and have proposed different end-time scenarios. Often history has proven them wrong. Some theories are built on multiple conspiracies that do not rise above the level of mere speculation. Here again we have more questions than answers, and we must confess with the apostle Paul: "For now we see only a reflection as in a mirror.… Now I know in part" (1 Corinthians 13:12).

**Humility**

I have chosen to call what we will attempt to do in this book an exercise in humility. We will, among other topics, discuss the human nature of Christ. Can we hope to understand Christ's humanness? Christ is fully divine, but, at the same time, He is also fully human. Through the ages theologians and church councils have tried to explain this mystery. Sometimes, I fear, they have not sufficiently recognized that they were dealing with things that have not been fully revealed. They have tried to reach a consensus about theological formulas in which they could express the inexpressible. They have, however, often forgotten that Christ is totally unique. There has never been one like Him, and there will never be another like Him! This means that we have no comparison. We stand before a deep mystery and that should make us humble.

Although we experience our own sinfulness and that of others every day of our lives, we must never forget that the problem of sin far exceeds anything we can understand and describe. When we are dealing with questions of sin, its origin, and its scope, we are confronted with what the Bible refers to as "the mystery of iniquity" (2 Thessalonians 2:7, KJV). The New Living Translation refers to the "lawlessness" that "will remain secret until the one who is holding it back steps out of the way." This realization should help us never to underestimate the nature of sin and the power of sin, and it should make us very reluctant to speak about overcoming sin and reaching the goal of perfection.

There is another aspect to remember. The very name "Last Generation Theology" indicates that it has to do with the end of time, more specifically with the short time just before the second coming of Christ. We certainly have received enough information to know that the end is coming. Christ is coming "soon" (although this word may to many of us seem somewhat elastic). There are signs that speak of the nearness and certainty of Christ's coming. Moreover, when we read the message of the Bible there cannot remain any doubt that there will be a climax in the confrontation between good and evil. The good news is that *good* will definitely and definitively triumph over *evil*. All this we do know. But there are many things we do *not* know. Apparently we are not meant to know everything in detail, and that may well be the main reason why God at times uses apocalyptic language, with its abundance of symbols and metaphors. Like an impressionistic picture, it paints its subject in broad strokes rather than in photographic detail.

Therefore, let us realize our limitations. One of the main problems I have with this Last Generation Theology is that it is so sure of itself. It seems to me that its proponents claim to know too many things with absolute certainty. And because the people who preach this theology are so certain that they are on the right track, they may easily be tempted to overlook elements that do not fit with their theory. In fact, that is what I believe is often happening.

**Caution**

A selective reading of the texts of the Bible and of statements found in the writings of Ellen White may seem to support the Last Generation Theology thesis, whereas looking at all the material leads, I believe, to a different conclusion. Therefore, before we delve into our topic for this chapter, let me make a few further introductory remarks. Seventh-day Adventists are adamant that their beliefs are based on the Bible. But most doctrinal discussions in the Adventist Church—at least at the more popular level—are usually also heavily sprinkled with statements from the pen of Ellen White. If there is any topic where this is the case, it is Last Generation Theology. Supporters and critics alike tend to base a major part of their arguments on comments that Ellen White made during her long ministry.

I want to use the Bible as my primary source in this book. I will quote Ellen White only sparingly in the main text, but will place a balanced selection of what she has said in an appendix to some of the chapters. I am convinced that the biblical evidence must take first place. After all, the first of the 28 Fundamental Beliefs of the Seventh-day Adventist Church states:

*In [his] Word, God has committed to humanity the knowledge necessary for salvation.* The Holy Scriptures are the supreme, authoritative, and the infallible revelation of His will. They are the standard of character, the test of experience, the definitive revealer of doctrines, and the trustworthy record of God's acts in history.[1]

The fundamental question is: how does Last Generation Theology fare in the light of the Bible? If we look at all the biblical evidence, do we find Last Generation Theology to be a truly biblical idea, or do we discover so many weaknesses or deficiencies in this belief that we must reject it and even warn against it? It is of critical importance that we try not to read our own preconceived ideas into the biblical text. Admittedly, that is far from easy, as we all read the Bible through lenses that are colored by our own background and our particular approach to the Bible. However, as we prayerfully read God's Word, we must do our best to clean our lenses and compare what we discover with what others have concluded from their reading.

A few basic rules must apply to our use of Scripture as we try to determine what the Bible says about the various aspects of Last Generation Theology. We must avoid a simplistic proof-text approach; that is, taking isolated texts out of their context and jumping from one text to another in our attempt to support a particular point of view. If we look at all the biblical material, we may find some texts that do not readily fit with the theory we are trying to prove, and we may easily succumb to the temptation to skip such passages or downplay their significance. We may find passages that, at least at first sight, seem to contradict each other. Will we try to force them

---
[1] The *Fundamental Beliefs* are found in many official documents of the Adventist Church, such as the *Church Manual*, 2015 edition.

into some harmonistic model, or can we live with the thought that it is all right if we don't understand everything and that many of our questions will, at least for now, remain unanswered?

I realize any Adventist discussion about Last Generation Theology cannot avoid mentioning some Ellen White statements. Some of these are at the very basis of Last Generation Theology. However, perhaps it should worry us that a belief that is so important to so many Adventist believers needs for many of its details so much support from a non-biblical source, and that its supporters seem to find it difficult to make a convincing case by just relying on the Bible. But considering that many will argue that the words of Ellen White, though not on the same level as the Bible, are also inspired and help us better discern what the Bible tells us, we will also refer to key Ellen White statements in the chapters that follow.[2]

In our use of what Ellen White has written, we should, at the very least, apply the same basic rules that we must also keep in mind when building our case from the Bible. In quoting Ellen White we must try not to be so selective that we only quote those statements that we find useful, while ignoring other statements. Moreover, we may find some contradictions and may simply have to conclude that Ellen White was not always totally consistent in what she said and wrote.

When we read the Bible we must not forget for what purpose the Bible was given—not as a textbook of history, geography, or physics, but as a guide for us in our relationship with God. Likewise, we must not expect Ellen White to deliver on things that were not part of the goals of her ministry. Her writings, Adventists generally believe, are given to help the church members in their spiritual experience, to

---

[2] In the footnotes I will refer to Ellen G. White as EGW and will only mention the name of the publication and the page numbers. All her publications may also be consulted online on the website of the Ellen G. White Estate.

guide the church through the complexities of its growth, and to avoid the pitfalls of the world in which it must operate and bear witness. It would be unfair to expect from Ellen White that she will provide us with complete theological models and in-detail developed theories. And yet, this is what is all too often done.

**It matters**

Some may ask, "Why pay so much attention to this particular theological trend? After all, theology is not a beta-science in which conclusions are supposed to be straightforward. Does it matter that some regard Last Generation Theology as an important 'truth' while others see it in quite a different light?" Yes, it does. It matters a great deal, because it touches on the basis of our relationship with God. It has a direct bearing on how we understand and experience our salvation—God's work of grace for us and our own role in it. And for many it may well be the difference between looking at their future with fear or with hope and confidence!

# Chapter 2

# Last Generation Theology: What it is and Where it Came From

Milian Lauritz Andreasen was born in 1876 in Copenhagen, Denmark. At age 15 he moved with his parents to Canada, where he trained as a tailor. A few years later Andreasen moved once again, this time to the United States. A short time after his arrival in the U. S. he came in contact with the Adventist faith and was baptized.[1] Soon he was active in the church, and after a few years he became a church worker. Initially he had little formal education, but eventually he attended Nebraska University, where in 1922 he earned a graduate degree. His career was a mixture of teaching, preaching, writing, and church administration. After having served as a church administrator at various levels, he became a General Conference Field Secretary (1941-1950), while also teaching at the Washington-based Seventh-day Adventist Theological Seminary (1938-1949). He wrote some 15 books, some of which have remained

---

[1] For detailed information on the life of M.L. Andreasen, see Virgina Steinweg's biography of Andreasen: *Without Fear or Favor* (Washington, DC: Review and Herald Pub. Assn., 1979).

influential. His "theology dominated Adventism from the 1940s to the late 1950s."[2]

An important event in Adventist theological history was the 1957 publication of the book *Seventh-day Adventists Answer Questions on Doctrine*.[3] The "questions" the title of this book refers to were asked by two non-Adventist evangelical leaders—Donald G. Barnhouse and Walter Martin—and were answered by a few key Adventist theologians: LeRoy E. Froom, W.E. Read, and R.A. Anderson. When the "answers" were subsequently to be published in this book, the manuscript was circulated for critical review to some 250 church leaders around the world. Rather surprisingly, M.L. Andreasen was not asked for comments.

Once the book came off the press a fierce controversy erupted between Andreasen and the leadership of the denomination, as the former took issue with a number of the "answers," in particular with regard to the doctrine of the atonement and the book's explanation of the human nature of Christ. Andreasen felt that, though the book contained "many good things," the section on the atonement was "utterly unacceptable."[4] The controversy ran so high that it even led to a temporary suspension of Andreasen's ministerial credentials (1961-1962).[5]

### "The Last Generation"

Andreasen's most important book, *The Sanctuary Service,* offers a detailed explanation of the scope and meaning of the sanctuary ritu-

---

[2]George R. Knight, *A Search for Identity: The Development of Seventh-day Adventist Beliefs* (Hagerstown, MD: Review and Herald Pub. Assn., 2000), p. 149.
[3]*Seventh-day Adventists Answer Questions on Doctrine*, annotated edition, with historical and theological introduction by George R. Knight (Berrien Springs, MI: Andrews University Press, 2003).
[4]M.L. Andreasen, "The Atonement," Nov. 4, 1957, cited in QOD, p. XXVI.
[5]See Roy Adams, *The Nature of Christ: Help for a Church Divided Over Perfection* (Hagerstown, MD: Review and Herald Pub. Assn., 1994), pp. 44-46.

al. The final chapter is entitled "The Last Generation." It is the classic description of what this term is about.[6] Adventist church historian George R. Knight provides a helpful summary of the basic concepts underlying the thinking of Andreasen.

- There is a parallel between the cleansing of the heavenly sanctuary and the cleansing of the "soul temple."
- The "last generation" will have to live through the "time of trouble" (just before Christ's second coming) without a Mediator. This idea is based on a number of statements found in books by Ellen G. White, notably in *The Great Controversy* and *Early Writings*.
- A crucial argument is derived from Ellen White's book *Christ's Object Lessons*, p. 69: "Christ is waiting with longing desire for the manifestation of Himself in His church. When the character of Christ shall be perfectly reproduced in His people, then He will come to claim them as His own."
- Jesus became incarnate in *post-fall* human nature. As time passed Andreasen would increasingly emphasize this point.
- The "last generation" will vindicate God's character before the universe.
- The atonement remained unfinished on the cross. It consists of three phases: 1) Christ's sinless life; 2) Christ's death on the cross; 3) Christ's ministry in the heavenly sanctuary, including the "perfecting of the saints" in the final moments of earth's history.[7]

In the first paragraph of chapter seven of *The Sanctuary Service* Andreasen neatly summarizes his view:

---
[6]M.L. Andreasen, *The Sanctuary Service* (Washington, DC: Review and Herald Pub. Assn., 1947, second edition), pp. 299-321.
[7]George R. Knight, *A Search for Identity*, pp. 144-147.

The final demonstration of what the gospel can do in and for humanity is still in the future. Christ showed the way. He took a human body and in that body demonstrated the power of God. Men are to follow His example and prove that what God did in Christ, He can do in every human being who submits to Him. The world is awaiting this demonstration (Romans 8:19). When it has been accomplished, the end will come. God will have fulfilled His plan. He will have shown Himself true and Satan a liar. His government will stand vindicated.[8]

According to the Bible, Andreasen continues, the demand for holiness is indisputable. The plan of salvation not only includes forgiveness of our sins, which neutralizes "the effect of sin," but it also includes sanctification, which is "a restoration of power for complete victory" over sin.[9] This sanctification "is not the work of a day or of a year but of a lifetime."[10] But complete victory over sin, difficult though it may seem, is possible, and just before the coming of Christ it will become a reality in "the last generation."

Thus it shall be with the last generation of men living on the earth. Through them God's final demonstration of what He can do with humanity will be given. He will take the weakest of the weak, those bearing the sins of their forefathers, and in them show the power of God. They will be subjected to every temptation, but they will not yield. They will demonstrate that it is possible to live without sin—the very demonstration for which the world has been looking and for which

---
[8] M. L. Andreasen, *The Sanctuary Service*, p. 299.
[9] *Ibid.*, p. 300.
[10] *Ibid.*, p. 301.

> God has been preparing....
>
> The last year of the conflict brings the final test.... The plagues fall, destruction is on every hand, death stares them in the face, but like Job they hold fast their integrity. Nothing can make them sin.[11]

Andreasen emphasizes that "the last generation" is not just about individuals: the men and women who live at the very end of time. We must see this in the context of the great controversy between Christ and Satan, which started with a war in heaven. When the devil was no longer welcome in heaven, the earth became his focus in stirring up rebellion against God. He succeeded in winning the trust of the first human beings and in making them sinners. And his attempts to create havoc and to fight God in the great cosmic conflict have been going on ever since.

> To remove every doubt in the minds of the angels—and later of man—God must let Satan go on with his work.... For the last six thousand years he has been giving the universe a demonstration of what he will do when he has the opportunity.
>
> This demonstration has been permitted to continue until now. And what a demonstration it has been! [12]

But the moment comes when "the demonstration must be completed." This is when "the last events are taking place,"[13] and in "a little flock" of "faithful witnesses" God's "power unto sanctification

---
[11]*Ibid.*, pp. 302-303.
[12]*Ibid.*, pp. 305-306.
[13]*Ibid.*, p. 306.

will stand fully revealed."[14] It will conclusively prove that Satan's accusation that God's law cannot be kept is totally false. It will not be easy. "God's people in the last days will pass through an experience similar to Job's."[15] They are referred to in the book of Revelation as the 144,000. "They will reflect the image of God fully. They will have disproved Satan's accusation against the government of heaven."[16] Satan cannot make them sin. "They stand the test, and God puts His seal upon them."[17]

### A.R. Jones, E.J. Waggoner, and W.W. Prescott

One of the basic issues underlying Last Generation Theology is the question of the human nature of Christ. What kind of human nature did Christ take upon Himself when He "became flesh"? Did His human nature resemble that of Adam and Eve *before* their fall? Or did He, as far as His humanity was concerned, become like Adam and Eve *after* their fall? In other words: was His human nature without our inherited tendencies towards evil, or did He share in those propensities? This is a much more important question than many may be aware of. It is not a matter of theological hair splitting; it has a major impact on how we think about a number of important points of doctrine. If Christ shared in our post-fall human nature, and therefore had in all respects the same kind of humanity as we have, we have no valid excuse not to reach perfection. Christ remained sinless, while He was completely like us. So, He may expect us also to reach for nothing less than sinlessness and a perfect character.

In today's Adventism we find two competing viewpoints. The

---
[14]*Ibid.*, p. 303.
[15]*Ibid.*, p. 314.
[16]*Ibid.*, p. 315.
[17]*Ibid.*, p. 319.

majority view is still that Christ took the kind of humanity the first human beings had *before* they disobeyed God and became sinful. This view is defended in the book *Questions on Doctrine*, which, in spite of the controversies it engendered, has been highly influential. Article five of the *Fundamental Beliefs* of the Adventist Church is inconclusive about this important point, but a semi-official, and widely distributed, commentary on the *Fundamental Beliefs* clearly tends towards a pre-fall view.[18] And the *Handbook of Seventh-day Adventist Theology*—another important document that outlines Adventist theology in considerable depth—emphasizes the uniqueness of Christ's human nature. "His humanity did not correspond to Adam's humanity before the Fall, nor in every respect to Adam's humanity after the Fall."[19]

The other view is that of Andreasen and others, and its popularity seems on the increase. Before the 1950s it was never a major issue in the Adventist Church, until it became so in Andreasen's days and beyond. But although Andreasen's name is forever connected with the view that Jesus took post-fall human nature, it was not a totally new idea that had never been heard before. In the writings of some of the early Adventist leaders—for example, Joseph Bates, James White, Stephen Haskell, and D. T. Bourdeau—we find references to the main elements of Last Generation Theology.[20] But Andreasen was mainly influenced on this point by a number of somewhat later prominent Adventist theologians: A.T. Jones (1850-1923), E. J. Waggoner (1855-

---

[18]*Seventh-day Adventists Believe* (Silver Spring, MD: Ministerial Association, General Conference of Seventh-day Adventists, 2005, second edition.), p. 59: "Christ veiled His divinity with the garb of humanity.... Christ's humanity alone could never have endured the deception of Satan....He was able to overcome sin because He relied completely on the Father...and 'divine power, combined with humanity, gained in behalf of man an infinite victory.'"
[19]Raoul Dederen, ed., *Handbook of Seventh-day Adventist Theology* (Hagerstown, MD: Review and Herald Pub. Assn., 2000), p. 164.
[20]See http://advindicate.com/articles/2017/5/21/five-popular-myths-about-last-generation-theology.

1916), and W.W. Prescott (1855-1944).[21]

The names of Jones and Waggoner may well be among the ten best known in Adventist history. The two men played a major role in the pivotal General Conference Session of 1888, where they championed—with the full support of Ellen White—the cause of righteousness by faith and advocated full reliance on divine grace in the salvation process rather than relying also on our own works. W.W. Prescott was a prominent Adventist educator and held several high posts in the church's administration. He also assisted in editing the 1911 edition of Ellen White's *The Great Controversy*.

It was not until a few years after the historic 1888 General Conference in Minneapolis that Jones began to develop and emphasize his views on the human nature of Christ. He wrote about it in his book *The Consecrated Way to Christian Perfection* (1905),[22] but his fullest exposition of the topic was in a series of lectures during the 1895 General Conference Session. By 1895 Jones was convinced that there was no difference whatsoever between Christ's human nature and ours.[23] The *Bulletin* of the 1895 General Conference abounds with statements by Jones that Christ assumed post-fall humanity and that this included all the evil propensities that human beings since Adam and Eve have been subjected to.[24] Here is just one sample, but many similar statements could be quoted:

> Unless he [Christ] was placed in a position as trying as that in which Adam stood, he could not redeem Adam's failure. If

---

[21]For more information about the pre-1950 views on Christ's humanity, see Ralph Larson, *The Word Was Made Flesh: One Hundred Years of Seventh-day Adventist Christology 1852-1952* (Fort Oglethorpe, GA: TEACH Services, Inc., 1986).

[22]Republished in 2017 by Glad Tidings Publishers (Berrien Springs, MI).

[23]George R. Knight, *From 1888 to Apostasy: The Case of A.T. Jones* (Hagerstown: MD: Review and Herald Pub. Assn., 1987), p. 136.

[24]See http://documents.adventistarchives.org/Periodicals/GCSessionBulletins/GCB1895-01-13ex.pdf.

man has in any sense a more trying conflict to endure than had Christ, then Christ is not able to succor him when tempted. Christ took humanity with all its liabilities.[25]

Ellet J. Waggoner also began to give prominence to his views about the humanity of Christ in the years following 1888. He agreed with Jones that "Christ's human nature inherited all the tendencies of sin and sinful passions common to all men."[26] He wrote in 1889: Children "are born with sinful tendencies, owing to the sins of their ancestors. And when Christ came into the world, he came subject to all the conditions to which other children are subject."[27] The fact that Christ could, in spite of these sinful tendencies, remain sinless, led Waggoner increasingly towards adopting a kind of perfectionism, whereby believers could reach a state of sinless perfection at the close of probation and during the so-called time of trouble.[28]

Perhaps the most outspoken example of W. W. Prescott's view on the humanity of Christ is found in a sermon he preached at a camp meeting on October 31, 1895.

God made man a little lower than the angels, but man fell much lower by his sin. Now he is far separated from God, but he is to be brought back again. Jesus Christ came for that work; and in order to do it, He came, not where man was before he fell, but where man was after he fell.[29]

---
[25] *Ibid.*, p. 333.
[26] David P. McMahon, *Ellet Joseph Waggoner: The Myth and the Man* (Fallbrook, CA: Verdict Publications, 1979), p. 104. See also: Woodrow Whidden, *From the Physician of Good News to the Agent of Division* (Hagerstown, MD: Review and Herald Pub. Assn., 2008), pp. 196-198.
[27] E.J. Waggoner, "God Manifest in the Flesh," *Signs of the Times*, Jan. 21, 1889, pp. 38-39.
[28] Woodrow Whidden, *From the Physician of Good News to the Agent of Division*, pp. 207-208.
[29] See https://m.egwwritings.org/en/book/1623.2000136#153.

**Since the 1950s**

Ever since the middle of the last century there has been an ongoing controversy in Adventism about the human nature of Christ. The publication of *Questions on Doctrine* caused the fire that had been smoldering to re-erupt with great intensity. Andreasen and his supporters considered the position that was taken in this book regarding Christ's human nature as a complete "sellout by the Adventist leadership to the evangelicals and as a betrayal of historic Adventism."[30] The section of the book that deals with Christ's incarnation wants the reader first of all to understand that the union of divinity and humanity in Christ was absolutely miraculous. The Bible calls the fact that God was manifest in the flesh "the mystery of godliness."[31] It goes on to underline that in taking human nature Christ did in no regard share in man's sinfulness. There remained an essential difference between Christ's human nature and our humanness:

> [The human] weaknesses, infirmities, failings are things that we in our sinful, fallen natures, have to bear. To us they are natural, inherent, but when He bore them, He took them not as something innately His, but He bore them as our substitute. He bore them in His perfect, sinless nature.[32]

The "enemies" of *Questions on Doctrine*—perhaps with some justice—argued that the authors were quite selective, and even somewhat manipulative, in their use of the biblical material and the Ellen White statements.[33] In any case, this matter would remain a central

---

[30] George R. Knight, *A Search for Identity*, p. 167.
[31] *Questions on Doctrine*, annotated ed., p. 51.
[32] *Ibid.*, p. 56.
[33] *Ibid.*, pp. 520ff.

issue in the further development and propagation of Last Generation Theology.

It is difficult to gauge how broad the support for Last Generation Theology has been among the church's theologians and leaders through the years, and among church members in general. Robert Pierson (1911-1989) was one of the most outspoken representatives of Last Generation Theology since the days of Andreasen. He was the president of the General Conference from 1966 to 1979. When he assumed the presidency he was determined to do all he could to combat any "liberal" tendencies in the church, which, he believed, had received far too much space during the previous administration of the denomination.[34] He called untiringly for revival and reformation, and he constantly pointed the believers to the need for being ready for the final events and for living as victorious representatives of their Master. For this, he said, is what God expects of the final generation on earth.

Herbert Douglass (1927-2014) served the church as an educational leader and in editorial roles. In addition he was a prolific author. In his book *Messenger of the Lord* Douglas gives a very informative and balanced picture of the life and ministry of Ellen G. White.[35] Theologically he was on the conservative side of Adventism, which explains his association with some independent ministries, such as Weimar College and Amazing Facts. When he worked as associate editor of what is now known as the *Adventist Review*, he could freely write and publish editorial articles defending Last Generation Theology, since the chief editor, Kenneth Wood, was of the same opinion. Douglass' views were very similar to those of Andreasen, even

---

[34] See Reinder Bruinsma, *Facing Doubt: A Book for Adventist Believers "on the Margins"* (London, UK: Flankó Press, 2016), pp. 48-50.
[35] Nampa, ID: Pacific Press Pub. Assn., 1998.

though Douglass had never read Andreasen at this time of his life. Through his own study he came to the conclusion that, just as a seed grows from the seed to the stalk and then to the full grain, each generation of believers grows and develops until eventually there is a last generation that has achieved maturity and perfection. He called this the "harvest principle."[36] Under the pseudonym of Kenneth Gage he wrote an article for the clergy's journal *Ministry* in which he, at length and in depth, set forth his belief that Christ took post-fall human nature upon Him when He came to this earth.[37]

More recent influential advocates of Last Generation Theology include Dennis Priebe, Larry Kirkpatrick, and Kevin D. Paulsen, who through speaking tours and seminars, and especially through publications on the Internet, have disseminated their Last Generation Theology ideas. Stephen Bohr, Doug Batchelor, and quite a few other prominent pastors could be included in a list of current Last Generation Theology supporters.

In 2005 Kirkpatrick published his book *Cleanse and Close: Last Generation Theology in 14 Points*,[38] in which he presented "a consensus statement" by a number of current and retired denominational workers about the main aspects of Last Generation Theology. This document is said to be intended as a reinforcement of the official Adventist Fundamental Beliefs and not as a replacement.

It is interesting (and perhaps also alarming) to note that Last Generation Theology is nowadays very popular with a number of so-called independent ministries that have connections with the Adventist Church. Among these are ASI (Adventist-laymen's Services & Industries), GYC (Generation of Youth for Christ), Amazing Facts,

---

[36] See https://en.wikipedia.org/wiki/Herbert E. Douglass.
[37] See http://www.adventistreview.org/assets/public/news/2014-12/humanatureChristfallen.pdf.
[38] GCO Press, 2005.

and the radio and television organization 3ABN. One may wonder why Last Generation Theology is so popular on the "right" side of the church. Many supporters of Last Generation Theology will argue that the reason lies in the fact that the conservatives in the church represent true Adventism, of which the ideas of Last Generation Theology form an integral part. Is this indeed the case, or is Last Generation Theology a defective theology? We will see.

We have already noted that some prominent church leaders in the past have been supporters of Last Generation Theology, notably president Robert Pierson. There is reason to think that the current president of the Adventist denomination also leans in this direction. In his inaugural sermon during the General Conference Session in Atlanta (2010), Pastor Ted Wilson underlined the importance of Ellen White's statement in *Christ Object Lessons* about the perfect final generation—a statement we have already referred to above. In other sermons by Pastor Wilson important aspects of Last Generation Theology are included.

Wilson has, to my knowledge, so far avoided using the term Last Generation Theology, but he has gone on record as saying that he supports it in essence. When asked at a meeting of the Adventist Theological Society what he thought of "last generation theology," his answer was quite clear:

> Leaning completely upon Christ and His righteousness, we need to believe that Christ will give us victory over sin through His power and not our own power (Phil 4:13; Romans 12:1, 2).... As we consecrate ourselves to Christ and allow Him to work in us to stay close to Him and His Word, we can then realize that beautiful quotation from *Christ's Object Lessons*:

"Christ is waiting with longing desire for the manifestation of Himself in His church. When the character of Christ shall be perfectly reproduced in His people, then He will come to claim them as His own" (p. 69).

The character of Christ can only be perfectly reproduced in our lives when we lean completely on Christ alone.'[39]

---

[39] See https://www.facebook.com/PastorTedWilson/posts/924770757578817:0.

# Chapter 3

# What is Sin?

In the previous chapter we have seen that Last Generation Theology represents a theological stream of considerable significance within Adventism, both in the past and in the present. We are now ready to look more closely at the main elements of Last Generation Theology, but where do we start? It is tempting to begin with a discussion about the human nature of Christ, since Last Generation Theology makes some specific claims about the kind of human nature Christ took in His incarnation. And, of course, the idea that perfection is required of the final generation of believers, and that Christ will not return before that has become a fact, is also a very basic issue that we could start with. Is it possible for human beings to reach perfection? We might therefore begin our further study by trying to respond to that fundamental question. And I can think of other aspects of Last Generation Theology that we could start with.

I have, however, decided first of all to focus on the topic of *sin*. This concept affects all other aspects of Last Generation Theology. Was the human nature of Christ affected by Adam's sin? If so, in what sense did He take man's sinful nature? This is just one of the questions we must ask. If human beings are to overcome all sin and to reach sinless perfection, what are we really saying? What concept of sin underlies such a statement? And how are our relationship with God, our salvation, and our struggle with sin to be viewed against the backdrop of the great controversy? In what way are our sin and our victory over sin part of the great cosmic conflict between good and evil? Sin is indeed a key element in any discussion of Last Generation Theology.

**The human predicament**

In his book *A Search for Identity*, George Knight mentions a few very serious flaws in Last Generation Theology. He identifies its inadequate doctrine of sin as one of these.[1] I fully share his conclusion. It is of utmost importance to have a good perception of what sin is before we proceed any further.[2]

"Sin" is one of those common words that have suffered from constant devaluation. People use it in all kinds of settings and at times even attach the positive connotation of adventure and fun to it. Often it is especially linked to exciting sexual behavior or to various forms of overindulgence, which may be unwise but are nonetheless painted as understandable or even enjoyable.

For many, sin is no longer a relevant idea. They say sin no longer exists, because they have ceased to believe in a God who condemns sin. Christians must protest against this line of thinking. They know that sin is at the bottom of all our problems and constitutes the root cause of all the troubles of our world. Paul Tournier (1898-1986), a famous Swiss physician and author with special expertise in pastoral counseling, once stated it well in just a few words: "There are no problems, there are only sins."

---

[1] George R. Knight, *A Search for Identity*, p. 150.
[2] Parts of this chapter are based on the section about "sin" in my book *Keywords of the Christian Faith* (Hagerstown, MD: Review and Herald Pub. Assn., 2008), pp. 64-73.

Therefore, before we focus on other issues, we must ask what is the true meaning of the term, how does the Bible define sin, and what does it mean to the Christian who seeks to emulate the Sinless One?

**Terminology**

Most Christians cannot read the Bible in its original languages (Hebrew, Greek, and a few short sections in Aramaic). But, fortunately, the Bible has been translated into thousands of different languages, and many excellent translations are readily available in all major languages. Without any study of the ancient languages we can have ample access to the Word of God. Occasionally, however, it is a bonus, even for non-theologians, to have some idea of the original words that are behind the words we find in the Bible in our language. That is certainly true when we deal with this rather generic word: *sin*. In the original languages we find a number of different words that are normally translated as *sin* but have different shades of meaning and express different aspects of sin.[3]

Four Hebrew words catch our attention. Firstly, there is the word *pesha*, which means rebellion, revolt. This is what sin is: rebellion, a rejection of God's directives, a "deliberate, premeditated, willful violation of a norm or standard."[4] The second word, *chataah,* is best translated as missing the mark, not reaching the goal, falling short. It suggests that sin not only includes wrongful actions but also covers the idea that we are not what we should have been. Sin is falling short of God's standard. In addition, we have the word *awon*, which means something like crookedness, straying from the right track. We also have the word *remiyyah*, which has the connotation of deceit and self-deceit.

---
[3]For a good summary of the use and meaning of the various Hebrew and Greek terms, see John M. Fowler, "Sin" in *Handbook of Seventh-day Adventist Theology*, pp. 237-239.
[4]*Ibid.*, p. 238.

The New Testament likewise uses several different words to refer to sin.[5] *Hamartia* occurs some 175 times; its literal meaning is missing the mark, as in target practice. In the New Testament it has the connotation of deliberate failure to attain God's standard. *Parakoé* is best translated as unwillingness to hear, and the word *parabasis* as to pass beyond, enter into forbidden territory. *Anomia*, a word that is used fewer times, is based on the Greek word for law (*nomos*) and suggests violation of the law.

None of these various terms refer to sin as an unfortunate weakness for which humans cannot be held responsible. They all suggest in different ways that sin is rebellion against the Lordship of God—a refusal to accept His authority over our life and destiny, and being less than we ought to be.

**What is sin?**

Sin is defined in the Bible as opposition to the law of God (1 John 3:4). This makes it, at first sight, rather simple: We must consult the divine law and whatever is not in agreement with it is sin. But what law does this statement refer to? Only to the Ten Commandment law? Or is there a broader application, to other laws and injunctions? Responding to that question may require a lengthy discussion about which categories of Old Testament law still apply to Christians who live in the 21st century. But even if we focus specifically on the Ten Commandments, things are not as straightforward as many tend to think. What, for instance, are the implications of Jesus' teachings? Did He not tell His disciples that the impact of this divine law extends far beyond the immediate literal application, including our inner motives as well? As we have already noted, in the Bible sin is not

---

[5]*Ibid.*, pp. 238, 239.

limited to wrong actions. In view of the interpretation Jesus gave to several commandments, we discover there can be sin even before we have actually done anything. Sin also has to do with what happens in our minds. Adultery, for instance, is not just having an affair or a one-night stand with someone we happen to meet at a party. Jesus says, "I tell you that anyone who looks at a woman lustfully has already committed adultery with her in his heart" (Matthew 5:28).

Other issues may be even more difficult to handle. We realize that theft is wrong, or "sinful," as a Christian would say. If I steal an expensive BMW because I am not content with the modest Citroen I have, I commit a sin. If you steal $100,000 by defrauding the company for which you work, you are a thief. But what if someone has absolutely no money (through no fault of her own) and takes a loaf of bread, simply to stay alive? Does that act of desperation also qualify for the word sin? And what if someone is a kleptomaniac, who is utterly unable to resist the impulse of stealing? He is not stealing because he wants to have all kinds of luxury items; he takes small things, often of little value, forced by some strange, inner compulsion that is beyond his control. Does that make this person a thief, or is he rather a patient in need of therapy?

Murder is usually considered the worst possible type of sin. In our scale of values, there is a wide chasm between telling a white lie and willfully stabbing our neighbor to death after a confrontation about the amount of decibels coming from the speakers in his house. But is physical violence in principle more objectionable than verbal abuse? And would murdering two people be intrinsically more evil than killing just one person? Is a serial killer more evil than someone who killed just once or twice? Or could the mass murderer be actually less culpable if it is established that he suffers from some inner compulsion that has starkly reduced his personal responsibility?

*What is sin?* Whatever else it is, it is the rupture in relationships. The Genesis story of the fall tells us that the first sin caused a sense of distrust between the first humans and their God. Adam and Eve hid from God (Genesis 3:8) and Adam admitted: "I was afraid" (3:10). Sin also brought an immediate physical estrangement between Adam and Eve and even between the first couple and their environment. In a dramatic way sin tragically disturbed the originally perfect relationships. Moreover, the Genesis story suggests that somehow human sin drastically affected the environment and even the animal world. This raises lots of difficult questions, but it is a clear warning against a too simplistic view of sin.

**Original sin**

Other questions arise as soon as we begin to think about sin. Is there something called "original sin," or "hereditary" or "ancestral" sin? This concept has found its way into Christian theology. It refers to the general condition of sinfulness into which all human beings are born, rather than to actual acts of sin committed by individuals. One might compare original sin to a virus that has stealthily infected the world after the first human couple fell into sin. Church father Augustine, and others after him, suggested that infant baptism is required to deal with the lethal result of original sin. If an unbaptized child dies, he said, it is destined for hell because of its inherited sinful condition. Apart from the fact that this view of hell sadly lacks biblical substance, Augustine's concept of original sin also had other indefensible elements. Nevertheless, the question remains: Why do we start out in life with a serious disadvantage because of the mistake of our first parents? What justice is there in the fact that Adam's sin brought not only death for himself but also that, as a result, death spread to everyone? Adam's "one trespass resulted in condemnation for all people" (Romans 5:12, 18). How fair is this?

Questions abound and several more could be added to those already posed in the previous paragraph. The text just quoted from Romans 5 suggests a principle of causality. One thing is caused by the other, and thus a chain of events is set in motion. One sin tragically led to universal sin, and universal sin led to universal death. That seems the inescapable message of the biblical narrative. Yet we must be careful not to talk only in terms of causality, as if every specific problem, and every specific case of human suffering, is caused by an identifiable sin on the part of a specific individual. Remember the biblical story of the man who was born blind? Jesus' disciples, who were used to thinking in terms of cause and effect, asked, "Rabbi, who sinned, this man or his parents, that he was born blind?" (John 9:2). Jesus told them not to come to any rash conclusions. "Neither this man nor his parents sinned.... This happened so that the works of God might be displayed in him" (verse 3). This same truth was also underlined when Jesus referred to an incident that had caused the death of 18 men. The tower of Siloam had caved in and had buried 18 victims under its debris. "Do you think they were more guilty than all the others living in Jerusalem?" Jesus asked (Luke 13:4). Clearly Jesus did not want people to draw this conclusion and link the accidental death of these 18 people with any specific sinful behavior.

And then we find the ominous statement in the Ten Commandments where God says He will punish "the sin of the parents to the third and fourth generation" (Exodus 20:5). How does this harmonize with the assuring words of the prophet Ezekiel, when he answered the question: "Why does the son not share in the guilt of his father?" The prophet leaves those who came with that question in no doubt: No! he says. "The child will not share the guilt of the parent.... The righteousness of the righteous will be credited to them, and the wickedness of the wicked will be charged against them" (Ezekiel 18:19-20).

Things are complex indeed. Bad things happen to bad people, but they happen to good people as well. Bad things do not just *happen*, they are a fact of life! That is the core issue with respect to the controversial concept of original sin.

> Once [sin] entered the sphere of human existence, there is no escaping its influence.... No Christian belief has more practical evidence to support it than this one.... Sin affects human nature, not just behavior. It is a basic condition of our existence and has an influence on everything about us.[6]

In discussing the sinful condition of man, theologians often use the term "total depravity." It emphasizes the devastating effect sin has on everything about us. There is nothing it does not touch, defile, and eventually destroy. The Swiss Reformer John Calvin expressed it in these powerful words: "The whole man is overwhelmed—as by a deluge—from head to foot, so that no part is immune from sin and all that proceeds from him is to be imputed to sin."[7]

Romans 5:12-19 is a key passage in this connection. It tells us that when Adam sinned, sin entered the entire human race. Adam's sin brought death, so death spread everywhere. Adam's one sin brought condemnation for all people. Paul does not explain *how* sin was transmitted from Adam to his posterity. The main point is this: Sin brings

---
[6] Richard Rice, *The Reign of God: An Introduction to Christian Theology from a Seventh-day Adventist Perspective* (Berrien Springs, MI: Andrews University Press, 1997, second edition), pp. 147-148.
[7] Quoted from Calvin's *Institutes of the Christian Religion*, II, i, 9, in: Rice, p. 147.

separation between God and humanity. "Because of Adam's sin, we have inherited this separation from God and more—a propensity to sin, wrongful tendencies, perverted appetites, debased morals, as well as physical degenerations."[8] We are not born morally neutral, but every person has an inborn "bent" towards evil.[9] We will hear more about this, since the crucial question in connection with Last Generation Theology is whether or not this propensity towards sin was also part of Christ's human nature.

The church father Augustine was of the opinion that sexual intercourse was the *modus operandi* in the transmission of original sin. His negative view of sex was to have an enormous influence on millions of Christians in the centuries to follow. There is, however, nothing in Romans 5, or in other texts, to support this unfortunate idea. The text intends to impress us with the fact that sin is very real, but the same passage also stresses the glorious fact that God is willing to accept us, nonetheless, as a result of the intervention through His Son.

Augustine is on safer ground when he tries to describe "original sin" in three terms that we find easy to understand. Sin, he says, is like a hereditary disease that is transmitted from one generation to the next. Sin also is like a power that holds us imprisoned, and we have no chance to free ourselves with our own power. And, thirdly, sin is like a debt that is passed from one generation to the next.[10]

## Personal and corporate sin

There is personal sin, and there is also corporate sin. Sin has infected the world and, as a result, the world is subject to death and

---

[8] John M. Fowler, "Sin" in *Handbook of Seventh-day Adventist Theology*, p. 237.
[9] George R. Knight, *Sin and Salvation: God's Work for and in Us* (Hagerstown, MD: Review and Herald Pub. Assn., 2008), p. 34.
[10] Alister McGrath, *Christelijke Theologie: Een Introductie* (Kampen: Uitgeverij Kok, 1997), p. 384.

decay. Mankind has become enslaved to sin (see Romans 6). The apostle Paul states that God's entire creation suffers from the effects of sin and that sin therefore has a cosmic dimension. "We know," the apostle Paul affirms, "that the whole creation has been groaning as in the pains of childbirth right up to the present time" (Romans 8:22).

There is a definite link between individual and corporate responsibility. Because many of us, as individuals, make wrong choices, countless events in the world take a certain turn and a kind of society develops in which man, rather than God, is the measure of all things. Because lots of men and women all around the world do not control their greediness and egotism, the world is infested with gross materialism and debilitating self-centeredness. And tragically, the kind of selfish and violent climate mankind has created will inevitably affect all who now are born into the world. And this lethal "cancer" of sin keeps on metastasizing and cannot be stopped.

We cannot merely blame our upbringing, the environment, our genes, or whatever else for what goes wrong in our lives. In the Bible sin is indeed described as an infection that has spread and now holds all of us captive. But that is not all that is to be said. The primary biblical definition of sin refers to conscious sinful behavior. "All wrongdoing is sin," we read in 1 John 5:17. Most Bible translations speak of unrighteousness as the main element of sin. When we sin we break the law of God (1 John 3:4). Sin is not disregarding some vague ideal or violating some general principle; it is nothing less than outright rebellion against the Ruler of the universe. This is what David recognized when he meditated upon his adulterous past: "Against you, you only, have I sinned" (Psalm 51:4).

Note that sin has to do with an act of will. It is acting against a norm, the absolute law of God. This differs radically from what most postmodern people believe. For them no absolute rules exist. We are, they maintain, only dealing with individual preferences and with a consensus that has developed in society. We may not like certain things, but that does not make them inherently evil. We may feel the need for personal growth and may regard some things in our own conduct as weaknesses that we would like to outgrow, but all this falls far short of the biblical view of sin as willful, active rebellion against an absolute norm given by a supreme divine Lawgiver. "Sin is the transgression of the law." Once again I quote 1 John 3:4, but this time from the old King James Version. This translation most poignantly underlines how God has defined a boundary for mankind. God says that sin is transgressing His holy, spiritual law (Romans 7:12-14). Breaking that law—crossing that divine boundary, the limit God set for us—is sin.

To the medieval Christian, seven sins were in a category of their own. These were the so-called "deadly sins," also known as the "cardinal" sins. These seven sins required special sacramental action if forgiveness and absolution were to be obtained. We meet these for the first time in a sixth-century list that originated with Pope Gregory the Great (c. 540-604): lust, gluttony, greed, sloth, anger, envy, and pride. Each of these sins corresponds with a particular virtue: chastity, abstinence, liberality, diligence, patience, kindness, and humility. There is no biblical foundation for a distinction between "cardinal" and lesser sins, the so-called "venial" sins. And this medieval list, and any other lists we might compile, of sins that supposedly are more serious than other wrongdoings, may mislead us more than they help, because they may suggest that there are actually sins that are not so very serious and also may lead us to forget that attitude and motive play an important role. The truth is: sin is always an utterly serious business.

### Sins of omission

A description of the phenomenon of sin is not exhausted by stating that sin is an act of willful transgression of a holy law, which has been revealed to us for our guidance through life. And it also goes beyond the cultivation of a desire to commit such a transgression, if we only had the courage to do so. James 4:17 adds a significant aspect: "If anyone, then, knows the good they ought to do and doesn't do it, it is sin for them." So, in addition to the sins of commission, there are sins of omission. Jesus' parable of Lazarus and the rich man (Luke 16:19-31) provides a prime example of this type of sin. The story tells us that the rich man bitterly complains about his fate in the hereafter to father Abraham, comparing his own misery to the bliss the poor beggar is experiencing. Abraham explains to the rich man that he could have done things in his earthly life that he failed to do. These omissions now come to haunt him. The parable of the sheep and the goats in Matthew 25: 31-46 contains the same lesson. When Jesus returns with His reward, things that we have failed to do may be the reason why we lose eternal life.

It takes but little thought to realize that all kinds of things happen because people fail to act. Edmund Burke's (Irish statesman and philosopher, 1729-1797) observation, "All that is needed for evil to triumph is for good people to do nothing," remains all too true. This further reminds me of the lines penned by the American poet Margaret E. Sangster (1838-1912):

> It isn't the thing you do, dear,
> It's the thing you leave undone
> That gives you a bit of a heartache
> At setting of the sun.

Yet, sin stretches even further. As we noted earlier, its meaning also covers the idea of missing the mark. This is the root meaning of one of the most frequently used Greek words (*hamartia*) and its Hebrew equivalents that are usually translated as *sin*. Jesus' words, "Be perfect, therefore, as your heavenly Father is perfect" (Matthew 5:48) continue to worry and confuse us. If the goal is to reach perfection, we seem indeed doomed to miss the mark. But this text must never be isolated from another key Bible verse: All have sinned; all fall short of God's glorious standard. But, it is added: We are all "justified freely by his grace through the redemption that came by Christ Jesus" (Romans 3:23).

Our falling short or missing the mark is a tragic reality we constantly experience in our daily lives. There are so many ways in which we fall short of the ideals we profess to uphold. There are so many ways in which we disappoint others and ourselves as we fail to keep promises that we should have kept and fail to attain goals that we should have reached. But when we feel frustrated by missing the mark and not reaching God's ultimate goal for us, we can be put at ease by what we read elsewhere in God's Word about our ultimate salvation through grace alone. "God saved you by his grace when you believed. And you can't take credit for this; it is a gift from God" (Ephesians 2:8, NLT).

**The reality of sin**

There is no doubt that sin is a crucial theme in the Christian vocabulary. It must be taken with utter seriousness. Its stark reality may not be ignored or toned down. Naturally, we wonder about the origin of sin. The Genesis story of the fall tells us about the first human act of rebellion. It seemed like a minor thing: picking a fruit that looked appealing and appetizing. But it was nothing less than an overt act of rebellion. It was the first demonstration of human hubris, exchanging God's standards for our own.

How could it happen? Adam and Eve had been created with the freedom of choice. They could remain obedient or could choose to follow their own ways. They could listen to the voice of their Creator or to the deceptive suggestions of the evil one. Prior to the fall in paradise there had already been a heavenly confrontation between good and evil. A heavenly being had exercised his power of choice, had chosen to rebel, and had found a following among the angelic beings. There are a number of biblical passages that provide us with a glimpse of what happened (See Revelation 12: 7-13; Ezekiel 28: 12-19; Isaiah 14:12-14).

We cannot fully understand the *what* and *why* of this fall into sin. However much we contemplate, it remains, in a very real sense, a mystery. The term used in 2 Thessalonians 2:7 (KJV) is very apt: it is the "mystery of iniquity." Some theologians have rightly stressed the absurdity of sin. "Perfect beings did not want to accept the limitations of creatureliness, which ultimately led to infinite abuse, hate and even lust for the destruction of life" and revolt against God.[11] But mysterious though the origin of evil may be, it has proven to be extremely powerful. And as soon as man was created, Satan, the captain of the evil angels, did what he could to infect the newly created earth with the germ of sin—and with regrettable success.

The apostle Paul wrote to the believers in Ephesus about the dark, evil forces humankind has to contend with: "Our struggle is not against flesh and blood, but against the rulers, against the

---

[11] Cornelis van der Kooi and Gijsbert van den Brink, *Christian Dogmatics: An Introduction* (Grand Rapids, MI: William B. Eerdmans Publishing Company, 2017), p. 317.

authorities, against the powers of this dark world and against the spiritual forces of evil in the heavenly realms" (Ephesians 6:12). We are not dealing with fictional horror stories or medieval superstition. This text refers to the cosmic battle that Adventists usually refer to as "the great controversy." It is about evil spirits under the command of the Satan.

At this point, we will not get sidetracked into all kinds of questions that emerge as soon as the name Satan is mentioned. One of the questions that invariably pops up is whether Satan is a power or a person. The answer depends on what we mean by the word "person." It has been suggested that the word "person" perhaps gives him too much honor. Sin is a parasitic phenomenon that feeds on what is good. It is not an independent power opposing God, but it is a parasite. And the devil may perhaps best be referred to as "anti-person" or "un-person," for want of a better word.[12] One thing must be emphasized above everything else: the great cosmic conflict, however real it is, must never be portrayed as an equal struggle between good and evil. "Jesus is the victor and has conquered the power of evil; that is the true state of affairs. All entities and powers are losers in view of the victory of Christ."[13]

This does not, however, take away from the undeniable fact that evil is a reality that demands a lifelong fight from all of us. It is a fight "against the super-personal aspects of culture, money, fashion, codes of behavior, cultural myths, public opinion, Western or Eastern ideals, national pride, social media, and so forth." In spite of their positive sides, "these powers also create addictions more than we often realize."[14]

---
[12]*Ibid.*, p. 334.
[13]*Ibid.*, p. 332.
[14]*Ibid.*, p. 323.

Our fight against sin, therefore, has super-human dimensions. In this struggle we need all the protection and tools we can possibly muster. We are admonished to "be strong in the Lord and in his mighty power." The advice is straightforward: "Put on the full armor of God, so that you can take your stand against the devil's schemes" (Ephesians 6: 10-11). Our fight is, first of all, against our personal sin. We may be struggling against our tendency to be rather economical with the truth. We may have the inclination to easily erupt in anger. We may sense the temptation of pride and prejudice. We may suffer from an addiction that, again and again, proves too strong for us to keep in check. Sin takes a multitude of forms. Once we truly realize this, we will cease to be judgmental about others, who may be struggling against different sins than we are up against.

We all have our own struggles. It has always been a mystery to me how some Christians have dared to come to the conclusion that they have fully mastered sin. 1 John 1:10 leaves us no room for that assessment: "If we claim we have not sinned, we are calling God a liar and showing that his word has no place in our hearts" (NLT). Christ spoke to us as much as He spoke to the Jewish leaders, who eagerly condemned the behavior of the woman who was "caught in the act," when He said, "Let any one of you who is without sin be the first to throw a stone at her" (John 8:7). Taking the full biblical definition of sin into consideration, we must strongly deny that in our present condition any of us can reach a state of sinlessness. "If we claim to be without sin, we deceive ourselves" (1 John 1:8).

Our fight against sin definitely includes recognizing the reality of corporate sin. Neither as individuals nor as a church community can we passively accept that our world is evil. We must use whatever influence we have to reduce the violence in this world and protest against the materialistic culture of waste and exploitation of our times. Christians cannot simply accept as a deplorable but unalterable fact that 12-year-old children are enlisted as soldiers, that women are beaten and abused, and that HIV sufferers do not get the medicines that science has made available. The conviction of Christ's soon return, when all evil will be finally eradicated, cannot lead to a complacent *laissez-faire* attitude and a refusal to help the hungry and needy as much as we can. The focus cannot just be on what a "last generation" must do; it must be on so much more! As long as we live in this world we must continue to be the light of the world and the salt of the earth (Matthew 5:13-16).

**How successful can we hope to be?**

The fight against sin is never fully over as long as we are citizens of this world. The fact that we will remain sinners as long as we live, however, does not mean that we cannot gain any victories. Christians know from experience that "there is power, power, wonder working power, in the precious blood of the Lamb."[15] We will speak about this in our next chapter, but let me say this now: *Overcoming sin is always a matter of grace.*

There are things that are expected of us if we want grace to have its influence on us, regardless of the generation to which we belong. For a start, we can determine to avoid compromising situations and to stay away from places or events that may tempt us to do something we know we should not do. If alcohol is a problem, we had better not frequent places where it is in ample supply. If Internet pornography is a temptation we struggle with, putting the PC in a place where all can see what is on the screen in front of us may be a useful preventive

---
[15] Lewis E. Jones, "There is Power in the Blood" (1899).

measure. If our fight is against laziness, we would do well to commit ourselves to some structured activity and ask someone to monitor us. We must try to replace activities that impact us in a negative way with activities that strengthen positive attitudes and awaken positive desires. "Do not be overcome by evil, but overcome evil with good" (Romans 12:21).

Sometimes outside help is needed. Overcoming certain addictions may well require specialized treatment. In addition to any willpower one may be able to muster, treatment is often needed to assist with giving a new direction to one's life. In general, encouragement from others can help us deal with our weaknesses. "There are 'friends' who destroy each other, but a real friend sticks closer than a brother" (Proverbs 18:24, NLT).

And then there is prayer. And, after that, still more prayer. Our daily prayer must be that we may be strong enough to not yield to temptation (Matthew 6:13). We must constantly ask God to help us with power to resist when temptation, often suddenly and unexpectedly, comes our way. We must pray for deliverance when the devil seeks to "devour" us (1 Peter 5:8), and pray that we may be able to persevere. And, of course, we should never forget to pray for forgiveness. And then for even more forgiveness!

**Guilt**

In closing this chapter, there is one further aspect that should be highlighted: Sin will keep raising its ugly head as long as we are in this world. But we do not need to continue to struggle with guilt. Our guilt can be taken away from us—totally. That is what atonement is all about. That is what it means when we say that we are saved. The fabulous truth is that there is a satisfying answer to the question once asked by the apostle Paul and repeated ever since by millions of Christians: "Oh what a miserable person I am! Who will free me from this life that is dominated by sin?" What better assurance is there than these words: "Thank God! The answer is in Jesus Christ our Lord" (Romans 7:24-25, NLT). The dilemma of sin can never be solved by human effort. But there is a solution. Thank God, we have a Savior. "Only in the cross can we see the depth of sin and the magnitude of the action to cure it."[16]

**Humility**

Much more could be said about sin. I hope, however, that our discussion in this chapter has been helpful in showing that sin is both simple and complex. Sin ruins relationships; it brings estrangement between human beings and, beyond anything else, also between us and our Creator. Sin has power over us. It imprisons and enslaves us. In summary: we are sinners. This seems pretty straightforward. God's Word is clear about the nature and dynamic of sin.

On the other hand, we are left with many unanswered questions. How could sin ever originate in a perfect universe? It is a mystery far beyond our comprehension. Sin has affected all of us, but why should that be? Why did God allow sin—and death—to spread to every human being? Why did He allow nature and animals to also be affected by the results of human sin? We know we are sinners, but in many ways we often do not realize the full extent of our sinfulness. We continue to discover new levels in our protest and rebellion against our creaturely limitations and realize ever more painfully that we sadly miss the mark in so many aspects of our life.

It is essential to study the topic of sin, but we must in all humility

---
[16] George R. Knight, *Sin and Salvation*, p. 43.

confess that there are many things we simply do not understand. That realization should make us very hesitant to make the kind of claims the supporters of Last Generation Theology are making, namely that it is possible to overcome sin and that, indeed, a group of people just before the end of time will reach a state of sinlessness. Could it be that the Last Generation Theology supporters do not have an adequate perception of the true nature of sin? And that they should humbly acknowledge that there are many things they simply do not know?

# APPENDIX

## Comments of Ellen G. White on Sin and Sinlessness[17]

### The Nature of Sin

Sin not only shuts away from God, but destroys in the human soul both the desire and the capacity for knowing Him. Through sin, the whole human organism is deranged, the mind is perverted, the imagination corrupted; the faculties of the soul degraded. There is an absence of pure religion, of heart and holiness.
*Prophets and Kings*, p. 233

The aggravating character of sin against such a God cannot be estimated any more than the heavens can be measured with a span. God is a moral governor as well as a Father. He is the Lawgiver. He makes and executes His laws. Law that has no penalty is of no force.
*Last Day Events*, p. 241

### The Origin of Sin

All sin is selfishness. Satan's first sin was a manifestation of selfishness. He sought to grasp power, to exalt self. A species of insanity led him to seek to supersede God. And the temptation that led Adam to sin was Satan's declaration that it was possible for man to attain to something more than he already enjoyed—possible for him to be as God Himself. The sowing of seeds of selfishness in the human heart was the first result of the entrance of sin in the world.
*Manuscript Releases*, vol. 7, pp. 232-233

---

[17]For a useful survey of Ellen White's views on the various aspects of sin, see Jiri Moskala, "Sin," in: Denis Fortin and Jerry Moon, *The Ellen G. White Encyclopedia* (Hagerstown, MD: Review and Herald Publishing Assn., 2003), pp. 1164-1176.

It is impossible to explain the origin of sin so as to give a reason for its existence.... Nothing is more plainly taught in Scripture than that God was in no wise responsible for the entrance of sin; that there was no arbitrary withdrawal of divine grace, no deficiency in the divine government, that gave occasion for the uprising of rebellion. Sin is an intruder, for whose presence no reason can be given.
*The Great Controversy*, pp. 492-493

### Sinful Propensities

Man was originally endowed with noble powers and a well-balanced mind. He was perfect in his being, and in harmony with God. His thoughts were pure, his aims holy. But through disobedience, his powers were perverted, and selfishness took the place of love. His nature became so weakened through transgression that it was impossible for him, in his own strength, to resist the power of evil. He was made captive by Satan, and would have remained so forever had not God specially interposed.
*Steps to Christ*, p. 17

# Chapter 4

# How Human was Christ? The Biblical Answer

The apostle John wrote his Gospel towards the end of the first century. Jesus called him to be His disciple while he was employed in the fishing company of his father. He was with Jesus during His earthly ministry. He stood at the foot of Jesus' cross, but he also saw the resurrected Christ with his own eyes. He proclaimed the gospel of his risen Lord. Towards the end of his long life he spent time in exile on the small Greek island of Patmos before his life ended in nearby Ephesus. This is his powerful testimony:

> In the beginning the Word already existed (John 1:1, NLT)… The Word became flesh and made his dwelling among us. We have seen his glory, the glory of the one and only Son, who came from the Father, full of grace and truth (John 1:14, NIV).

When John wrote these words, the apostle Paul had already written to the believers in Philippi about this same magnificent fact of Jesus' incarnation—God entering human flesh. For Paul this was the ultimate demonstration of humility.

> Though [Jesus] was God, he did not demand and cling to his rights as God. He made himself nothing; he took the humble position of a slave and appeared in human form. And in human form he obediently humbled himself even further by dying a criminal's death on a cross (Philippians 2:6-7, NLT 1990).

**Christology**

The miracle of Christ's incarnation demands our adoration prior to any attempts at understanding; it asks for worship before we engage in any theological reflection. Our study will not provide us with all the answers we may want to have. How can we ever fathom what this astounding and utterly unique event implies: Christ becoming one of us? How can we as painfully finite human beings grasp what exactly happened when divinity was clothed with humanity? Human language remains totally inadequate. It must be with this sense of humility that we embark in this chapter on our attempts to say something, in our pitifully insufficient human language, about the eternal Word becoming human flesh.

When Christ walked the roads of Palestine with His group of male and female disciples, preaching, performing miracles, talking, listening, eating, and associating with all sorts of people, many of His contemporaries sensed that He was different from other human beings. One of the first persons to notice this was His mother, Mary. She was amazed by many of the things she saw and heard, and she did not know what to make of them; however, she stored these things in her heart (Luke 2:51), until they might at some later point in time become clear to her. In the Gospels we hear people time and time again asking the question: "Who is He?" When they saw Jesus performing miracles, even bringing some dead people back to life, and heard Him making the claim that He could forgive people's sins, they wondered: "Who is this man?" (Luke 7:49). When Jesus asked His disciples what people were saying about Him, they reported a range of different answers: "Some say [you are] John the Baptist, some say Elijah, and others say Jeremiah or one of the other prophets" (Matthew 16:14, NLT).

Jesus is the central figure of the New Testament. The Gospels were written in response to the questions people with all sorts of different backgrounds had about Jesus. Mark in all likelihood recounted what he had heard from Peter, as he served as the apostle's translator. Matthew wrote for Jewish readers, and Luke for the "esteemed" Theophilus, while a few decades later John wrote for yet a different audience. The second book by Luke—the Book of Acts—relates how the apostles proclaimed the risen Christ on the basis of their experiences with Him. In the New Testament letters, Paul and others applied the teachings of Christ to the daily life of the believers in the churches that had been established. And the last Bible book is not the Revelation *of John*, but both the "revelation *from* Jesus Christ" (NLT), and the revelation *of* Jesus Christ (NRSV). As the apostles relived their experiences with their Lord and started pondering afresh Jesus' words and teachings, and as they saw how many Old Testament passages found their fulfillment in Chris, they laid the basis for the branch of theology that is commonly called Christology—the study of the doctrine of Christ.

In the earliest epoch of church history, the paramount issue was whether gentile Christians had to meet the same requirements for church membership as Jewish Christians. An agreement was reached during a meeting that has often been referred to as the first church council. Acts 15 tells us how a consensus was reached and communicated to the churches that had been established by the middle of the first century. But soon the focus of the early church shifted towards the relationship between God the Father and His Son, and also to their relationship with the Holy Spirit. Centuries of debate would lead the church to formulate the Doctrine of the Trinity. After long debates and fierce controversy, it was generally accepted that there is only one God but that the Godhead consists of three eternal and fully equal "persons": Father, Son, and Holy Spirit. The word "Trinity" is not found in the Bible; it was coined to describe the central mystery of the Christian faith.

If you want to study a complicated theological topic, get some handbooks on Christian doctrine and read the chapter on the Trinity. It is usually very heavy going! In many respects it is easier to grasp what the doctrine of the Trinity denies than what it affirms. It underlines that there is but one God and that we must not see the Father, the Son, and the Spirit as three separate gods. The doctrine also denies that the Son is lower in rank than God the Father and denies that He, at some point in the distant past, had a beginning. These two views were among the "heresies" that the church fathers vehemently rejected!

The topic of the Trinity must be approached with an attitude of deep humility. Who are we that we can define God? The very words we use are human words. Take, for instance, the word "person." What does it mean when we say that God is a person? Is His personhood similar to ours? The earliest theologians and church leaders, who spoke Greek and used that language in their writings, used the word *hypostasis*, which is much more vague and literally refers to an underlying reality. When Latin replaced Greek in the Western Church, the Latin word *persona* began to be used. The original meaning of this Latin word had, perhaps surprisingly, a link with the theater. A "persona" was a mask worn by the actors when they played a particular role. In English we have continued to use the term "person" when speaking of the three persons of the Godhead. Like the Greek- and Latin-speaking Christians, we have no adequate language at our disposal, and we should in all humility remember that it is for want of a better term that we still use the word "person."

**The two natures of Christ**

The other issue that kept minds and emotions occupied in early church history was that of the "nature" of Christ. This issue has special relevance for our discussion of Last Generation Theology. Already in New Testament times there were people who had questions about the deity of Christ, while others wondered about the true humanity of the Savior. The Gnostics, for example, were adamant that it would be impossible for a divine being—as a pure Spirit—to associate Himself with evil matter (human flesh)! They thought that in His incarnation Christ assumed a phantasmal, make-believe body. He only *appeared* to be a human being. In the latest strands of the New Testament we already find protests against this type of thinking. That is why John writes in his second general epistle: "Many deceivers, who do not acknowledge Jesus Christ as coming in the flesh, have gone out into the world." John has nothing good to say about people who spread this kind of teaching. Anyone who does this is a "deceiver and the antichrist" (2 John 7).

The debate about the nature of Christ was a major threat to the unity and well-being of the Christian church and also caused a tremendous amount of tension between different groups of believers. In the year 325 some 300 church leaders (bishops) accepted the invitation of the Roman Emperor Constantine to travel to Nicea (now Iznik in Turkey) for a meeting that was called with the intention of restoring the unity of the church. The Nicene Creed was the outcome of their deliberations. But this did not stop the disagreements once and for all. The formula that was agreed upon in Nicea was revised at another important church council in 451 in Chalcedon (also in Turkey, close to Constantinople), after several theories were being spread that raised many eyebrows. The text of the Nicene Creed about Jesus reads as follows:

> [We believe] in one Lord Jesus Christ, the Son of God, begotten of the Father [the only-begotten; that is, of the essence of the Father, God of God], Light of Light, very God of very God, begotten, not made, being of one substance with the Father; by whom all things were made [both in heaven and on earth]; who for us men, and for our salvation, came down and was incarnate and was made man; he suffered, and on the third day he rose again, ascended into heaven; from thence he shall come to judge the quick and the dead.[1]

I have quoted this text in full for a purpose. I am not going to attempt a detailed commentary and a full explanation of what all of this means, and neither will I discuss the various Greek words underlying this formula. I have cited it to demonstrate how difficult, apparently, it was to describe who and what Jesus Christ was. And it only gets more and more complex when we study the many dif-

---
[1] See J.N.D. Kelley, *Early Christian Creeds* (London: Longmans, Green and Co., Ltd, 1967 edition), pp. 205-262.

ferent so-called christological controversies about the two natures of Christ—how they were related and impacted each other. It is important to keep this in mind when we try to evaluate the biblical data concerning the natures of Christ, and of His human nature in particular. The prolonged and fierce debate and controversy of the early centuries should raise a red flag if any Seventh-day Adventist Christian (or anyone else, for that matter) proposes some simplistic, definitive definition of the human nature of Christ—usually on the basis of a selective reading of the biblical material and by combining some statements by Ellen White.

Before we move on to the relevant biblical data, a few words about Adventist history are in order. In the past the doctrine of the Trinity and the topic of Christology did not always get the attention of Adventist believers these subjects deserve. For a long time the emphasis was mostly on the special beliefs that set Adventists apart from other Christians, such as the Sabbath, the non-immortality of the soul, the heavenly sanctuary, a particular view of the thousand years of Revelation 20, the three angels' messages, and the interpretation of Daniel and the Revelation. In their views regarding the common Christian doctrines, the early Adventists stayed mostly by what they had learned in the denominations from which they had come. A few of our key leaders in the first decades of Adventism had their roots in the Christian Connection—a small movement in the so-called restorationist tradition. These restorationists wanted to restore what they saw as the original, biblical version of Christianity. One of their characteristics was that they rejected the doctrine of the Trinity, and those who had belonged to this group brought this conviction with them when they joined the Advent Movement. They also imported into Adventism the view that Christ was, in fact, a created being who was lower in rank than God the Father. These views have been rather tenacious, and even today a considerable number of Adventists (unfortunately) feel that the doctrine of the Trinity is a false teaching and that the approach to the natures of Christ that was espoused in the book *Questions on Doctrine* is a betrayal of original Adventist truth.

But let's now look at what the Bible tells us about the two natures of Christ. What we have said above should have made us aware that the matter may be much less straightforward than is often suggested. Be prepared to find not only "easy" texts but also statements that are difficult to understand and, possibly, also contain elements that may seem contradictory. If, after reading the rest of the chapter, you have a complete and perfect understanding of the topic of Christ's humanity, you would be the first person I know of who has succeeded in this respect. I must in all humility admit that I have indeed found some answers—enough answers to know that Jesus is my unique Savior—but that I am also left with many, many unanswered questions.

**What does the Bible say about Christ's divinity?**

The official Adventist teaching is that Jesus is fully God and fully man. *Fundamental Belief* number four begins with these words:

> God the eternal Son became incarnate in Jesus Christ. Through Him all things were created, the character of God is revealed, the salvation of humanity is accomplished, and the world is judged. Forever truly God, He became also truly human, Jesus the Christ. He was conceived of the Holy Spirit and born of the virgin Mary.

The words "fully God" imply that Christ has always existed. There never was a time when Christ was not. He is "with God" and He "was God" (John 1:1). Full divinity implies eternity. The Old Testament prophet Isaiah not only spoke of the child that was to be born as the "Prince of Peace," but also called Him "the Mighty God" and "the everlasting Father" (Isaiah 9:6). Peter confessed that Jesus was the Messiah, "the Son of the living God" (Matthew 16:16), and Thomas exclaimed, when looking into the eyes of the risen Christ, "My Lord and my God!" (John 20:28).

Together with the other members of the Trinity, Christ is the Creator of all that exists. Paul stressed that point in his letter to the church in Colossae: "For in him all things were created: things in heaven and on earth, visible and invisible" (Colossians 1:16). He is "the Amen…the ruler of God's creation" (Revelation 3:14). Life itself is in Him (John 1:4). Jesus has a "name that is above every other name" (Philippians 2:9). Numerous times Jesus is referred to as Lord. In the Septuagint, the Greek Old Testament (which was used in New Testament times), this word Lord (*Kurios*) was the title commonly reserved for God the Father. It is essential that we recognize Jesus Christ as the Lord. Paul asserted that if we confess with our mouth that Jesus is Lord we will be saved (Romans 10:9). And speaking of the return of Jesus Christ at the end of history, the same apostle wrote: "We wait for the blessed hope—the appearing of the glory of our great God and Savior, Jesus Christ" (Titus 2:13).

Because Jesus was fully God, the disciples did not just treasure His memory after He had ascended to heaven—"they worshiped him" (Luke 24:52). And even before this, Jesus had accepted worship from His followers. After Jesus had walked on water and climbed back into the boat, "the disciples worshiped him" (Matthew 14:33, NLT). And when Jesus had risen and appeared to His disciples, "they worshiped him" (Matthew 28:9, 17). For people with a Jewish background to worship any other being than the only God was an unthinkable abomination. There is an abundance of evidence that in the early church worship centered on the Lordship of Jesus Christ, and references to the hymns that were used in their worship testify to the belief of the early Christians that Christ was of equal status with the Father.[2]

**What does the Bible say about Christ's humanity?**

I could have quoted many more Bible texts that emphasize Christ's complete divinity. He is, indeed, our *Lord* and our *God*! But there is another side to the picture. *God became man.* And so we not only find passages in the New Testament that identify Jesus as God, we also read about the *man* Jesus Christ, as, for instance, in 1 Timothy 2:5: "For there is one God and one mediator between God and mankind, the man Christ Jesus!"

The men and women who associated with Jesus on a daily basis when He was among them had no doubt that, whatever He was, He was a human being in the full sense of the word. When, against the customs of His day, Jesus had asked a Samaritan woman to give Him a drink, she uttered her amazement with these words: "You are a Jew and I am a Samaritan woman" (John 4:9). This woman made an important point about Jesus' humanness. He looked like a "normal" Jew of His day. We have no portrait or selfie of Jesus, but of one thing we can be quite sure: He did not look like a blond Viking or a young, white American adolescent, such as we see on so many illustrations in children's Bibles and on posters.

Jesus was the Son of God. But He was also born of a human moth-

---

[2]Norman H. Young, "Jesus—Divinity Revealed in Humanity" in Bryan W. Ball and William G. Johnsson, eds. *The Essential Jesus: The Man, the Message, the Mission* (Boise, ID: Pacific Press Pub. Assn., 2002), pp. 116-119.

er (Galatians 4:4). Like every other human being, He had a body, a soul, and a spirit. When facing His imminent death, Jesus' soul was "troubled" (John 12:27), and when He was about to die He said: "Father, into your hands I commit my spirit" (Luke 23:46).

Jesus came as a baby and grew up as a normal child. Like any other human being, He could be hungry (Matthew 4:2) or thirsty (John 19:28). He needed sleep (Matthew 8:24) and could be tired (John 4:6). He knew of sadness, as the shortest text in the Bible tells us when reporting the death of Jesus' friend Lazarus: "Jesus wept" (John 11:35). And, of course, the ultimate proof of His humanness was that He could suffer and die.

A number of New Testament passages mention that Christ "took" human nature. Paul wrote that Jesus came in "human form" (Philippians 2:7, NLT). But in his letter to the Romans, the apostle is more specific: God "sent his own Son in a human body like ours—except that ours are sinful" (Romans 8:3, TLB). And the author of Hebrews agrees: "He had to be made like them, fully human in every way" (Hebrews 2:17). So, what does this "in every way" mean? It certainly means that He could be tempted as we are. He can understand our situation, the same author underlines, because He "has been tempted in every way, just as we are," with the infinite difference, that He never yielded to sin (Hebrews 4:15). Whatever may be said, and whatever questions may be asked about Jesus' human nature, one thing is clear: He never sinned!

### Did Jesus adopt a "sinful" human nature?

Jesus was fully man. But what about the aspect of sinfulness in which all human beings share? Did He also fully share in our human nature in that respect? He was tempted in all things like we are, but did He perhaps have an advantage by not having the same inherited inclination, or propensity, toward sin? Or must we conclude from words like "being in every respect like us" that He also shared in the sinful aspect of our nature that has, ever since Adam sinned, been passed on from one generation to the next? The biblical material is not so clear-cut as some want us to believe.

Romans 8:3 is a key verse. In the New King James Version, which is the favorite translation for most Last Generation Theology supporters, we read: "For what the law could not do in that it was weak through the flesh, God did by sending His own Son in the likeness of sinful flesh." Some commentators, however, point out that the "likeness" of sinful flesh does not necessarily mean the "sameness" of human flesh, with its inherited tendencies towards evil. Yet others contend that Romans 8 leaves us with the impression that Jesus' humanity did include the inherited propensities towards sin. Others again, however, feel that Hebrews 7:26 points us in another direction by affirming that Jesus was "separate from sinners."

Raoul Dederen, one of the most respected Adventist theologians, wrote in his chapter about Christ in the *Handbook of Seventh-day Adventist Theology*:

> He came "in the likeness of human flesh" (Romans 8:3). He took human nature in its fallen condition with its infirmities and liabilities and bearing the consequences of sin; but not its sinfulness, he was truly human, one with the human race, except for sin. He could truly say "He [Satan] has no power over me" (John 14:30).... Jesus took human nature, weakened and deteriorated by thousands of years of sin, yet undefiled and spotless. "In him," writes John, "there is no sin" (1 John 3:5).[3]

---

[3] Raoul Dederen, "Christ: His Person and Work," in *Handbook of Seventh-day Adventist Theology*, pp. 164-165.

### "Tempted in every way, like we are"

But, if Christ took human nature in the sense that Professor Dederen wrote in the statement I just quoted, how must we then understand the statement by the author of Hebrews that Christ was tempted in every respect like we are? Did He not have a tremendous advantage over us if He did not have the propensities toward evil, like those we have inherited from Adam? Can He really be our ultimate role model if He started at a different point from where we start in life?

What does Hebrews 4:15 really mean? Most readers will not take the text literally in the sense that Christ's temptations were *identical* to ours. That could hardly be the case. Contemporary life presents us with temptations earlier generations never knew. And there were, undoubtedly, temptations in the ancient world, in the Middle Ages, and even less than a century ago, that we no longer face. However, the urges and sensations behind our temptations have always existed, and in fundamental ways humanity has always faced similar temptations.

Christ's temptations were not make-believe pieces of theater. They were absolutely real (Matthew 4:1-11). And, yes, they were fundamentally the same as they were for the people who first read the book of Hebrews and as they are for us who live in the first quarter of the 21st century. But, even if we have the view that Christ took pre-fall human nature and did not have the same inherited propensities towards sin that we have, it does not follow that Christ had an advantage over us in His consistent rejection of sin. On the contrary, when we are confronted with major crises in our life, we must always react on the basis of our human limitations. Christ, however, remained God—even during His incarnation. At any moment He could have invoked His divine powers to save Himself from every predicament.

When Satan suggested to Jesus that He should throw Himself from the roof of the temple, Jesus could, indeed, have commanded a legion of angels to provide a soft landing in the temple court. But He knew that we would not have that possibility in similar circumstances. Had He succumbed to this temptation by calling upon divine resources that are not at our disposal, He would no longer have been our perfect example and could no longer be our Savior. "It seems from a simple reading of the Bible that irrespective of the constitution of his human nature, Jesus was tempted far beyond how any other person can ever be tempted. Most of his temptations are not even temptations to us, because we lack the ability to respond to them successfully."[4] The good news is: Jesus could have sinned when He was tempted, but He did not!

The pre-fall interpreters do not deny that Christ was subject to human weaknesses. His body was affected by the same bodily processes and the same physical challenges as the bodies of His contemporaries. "But they deny that Christ took or had sinful inclinations, propensities, or tendencies."[5] After a careful evaluation of viewpoints, Woodrow Whidden concludes:

> With all due respect to the mystery inherent in the sinlessness of the humanity of Christ, it seems best to sum up the issue in this way: according to Ellen White, Christ's humanity was affected by sin enough to identify sufficiently with sinful humans in their struggle with temptation, but was without the infection of sin to the degree that His sinlessness of nature enabled Him to offer a fully effectual sacrifice of atonement for penitent "true believers" and thus function as a duly

[4] George R. Knight, *Matthew: The Gospel of the Kingdom* (Nampa, ID: Pacific Press Pub. Assn., 1994), p. 69.
[5] Woodrow Whidden, "Humanity of Christ," in *The Ellen G. White Encyclopedia*, p. 694.

effectual divine/human intercessor.[6]

In one of his other books the same author makes this succinct but thoughtful statement:

> They [the expressions pre-Fall and post-Fall] are not very helpful, in that Jesus was neither completely pre-Fall nor post-Fall—as such terms would imply. On the one hand, He was pre-Fall in the sense that His humanity was not "infected" with sinful, corrupt tendencies, or propensities to sin, such as we are born with. On the other hand, He was post-Fall in the sense that His humanity was "affected" by sin, in which He never indulged.
>
> Thus He was neither completely one nor the other. In a very important sense He was both, and the all-or-nothing implications of such expressions are not helpful.[7]

In the next chapter we will try to give a fair representation of what Ellen G. White wrote on the topic of the nature of Christ's humanity. For Last Generation Theology supporters, the certainty that Christ took post-fall human nature rather than pre-fall human nature is an important building block for their theory. But it should be clear that this position is mainly decided by statements of Ellen G. White that are directly or indirectly related to this matter.

## The ultimate paradox: divinity and humanity combined

How Christ can at the same time be fully human and fully divine

---
[6] *Ibid.*, pp. 695-696.
[7] Woodrow Whidden, *Ellen White on the Humanity of Christ* (Hagerstown, MD: Review and Herald Pub. Assn., 1997), p. 15.

remains one of the great paradoxes the Christian believer is faced with. According to the *Cambridge English Dictionary*, a paradox is "a situation or statement that seems impossible or is difficult to understand because it contains two opposite facts or characteristics."[8] The doctrine of the Trinity presents us with such a paradox: God is one and God is three. I am convinced that these two elements are both true, even though it seems a logical impossibility. I must always keep both elements in balance. If I overemphasize the three-ness of God I am in danger of losing sight of His one-ness, and, on the other hand, I must not so interpret His one-ness that the three-ness evaporates.

Another example of a fundamental paradox in the Christian faith is the nature of the Bible—the written word of God. The Bible is God's word. But at the same time what we read in this sacred book are human words, written by people against the background of their own cultures, using their own words and writing style, and utilizing particular literary genres. Paradoxically, the Bible is both divine and human. Overemphasis on the human aspect will destroy the authority of the Bible. On the other hand, a lack of recognition of the human element will easily lead us to a distorted theory of inspiration.

What is true of the *written Word* also applies to the *living Word*. When dealing with the two natures of our Lord, we stand for the ultimate paradox. How can anyone be simultaneously fully divine and fully human? How are these two natures united—blended—in one Person? We tread on holy ground, a terrain full of pitfalls for finite human minds. If we focus on the divine nature of Christ only, we may unwittingly follow in the footsteps of the heretics of ancient times, who made His human nature into some kind of make-believe humanness. In other words, we accept the idea that He *appeared* to be

---

[8]See https://dictionary.cambridge.org/dictionary/english/paradox.

human; He *played the role* of a human being, but He never fully was one of us. If, on the other hand, we lay stress on His humanity to the extent that we lose sight of His full divinity, we end up with a Christ who has no life in Himself, and, as He cannot give what He does not possess, He cannot make us partakers of His eternal life. Thus, when we disturb the perfect balance between Christ's divinity and His humanity, we no longer have a true Savior.

Must we then leave our intellect behind when we contemplate this difficult topic? Must we be prepared simply to accept what many see as nonsensical statements? Or is this the place where, in all humility, we take off our shoes, recognizing that we tread upon holy ground, and where, aware of our creaturely finiteness, we reverently bow before the mystery that confronts us? Note that this is what Ellen White suggested in 1898:

> The humanity of the Son of God is everything to us. It is the golden chain that binds our souls to Christ, and through Christ to God. This is to be our study. Christ was a real man; He gave proof of His humility in becoming a man. Yet He was God in the flesh. When we approach this subject, we would do well to heed the words spoken by Christ to Moses at the burning bush, "Put off thy shoes from off thy feet, for the place where on thou standest is holy ground." We should come to this study with the humility of a learner, with a contrite heart. And the study of the incarnation of Christ is a fruitful field, which will repay the searcher who digs deep for hidden truth.[9]

The incarnation of Christ and the virgin birth are inseparably

---
[9] EGW, *The Youth's Instructor*, Oct. 13, 1898. Also found in *The Seventh-day Adventist Bible Commentary*, vol. 7A, p. 443.

connected concepts. There is enough historical evidence for the fact that a remarkable Jewish rabbi with the name Jesus did indeed live in Palestine in the first few decades of the Christian era. But there is, of course, no historical corroboration for the biblical story of the manner of His birth. We are told in the gospel story that a young woman named Mary became pregnant without having had sexual intercourse! For many, this idea of a virgin birth is totally preposterous. And, admittedly, many theological scholars also consider this story merely a pious myth. I am also puzzled how something so exceptional could have happened, but over time I have become satisfied with the thought that we should indeed expect something completely out of the ordinary to occur when divinity decides to come down to the level of humanity. Is it too much to expect something that is totally unique and extraordinary when God comes to live among us for some 33 years in the person of His Son Jesus Christ?[10]

Questions are often raised about the term "only-begotten," which is applied in a number of Bible translations to Jesus. Other translations prefer words like "only" or "one and only." The original Greek word is *monogenés* and is used nine times in the New Testament. We find it, for example, in John 1:18. The King James Version reads: "No man hath seen God at any time, the only begotten Son, which is in the bosom of the Father, he hath declared him." The Revised Standard Version renders it as: "No one has ever seen God; the only Son, who is in the bosom of the father, he has made him known." The term "only begotten" is an expression that indicates "in a very special manner, that which is unique and is incomparable in Christ."[11] *The Seventh-*

---
[10]Reinder Bruinsma, *Faith, Step by Step: Finding God and Yourself* (Grantham, UK: Stanborough Press, 2006), pp. 75-76.
[11]G.C. Berkouwer, *Studies in Dogmatics: The Person of Christ* (Grand Rapids, MI: William B. Eerdmans Publishing Company, 1954), p. 175.

day *Adventist Bible Commentary* explains the word *monogenés* along the same lines. It has nothing to do with status or order of birth but points to absolute uniqueness.[12] Experts in the Greek language leave us in no doubt. The true meaning of the word is: the only one of a kind, only, single, unique![13]

### The uniqueness of Jesus Christ

*Christ is unique.* There has never been one like Him. The biblical testimony underlines both His divine and His human nature. It is clear that Christ became fully man; He was like His contemporaries in Galilee and could blend into the crowds in Jerusalem. But He never sinned. Not once!

The New Testament "was not consumed with theological speculation about the divine and the human natures in Jesus. Statements about Jesus' person came indirectly in the context of worship and pastoral exhortation." Perhaps we would have liked the New Testament to be more specific and systematic in its witness regarding the divine and the human natures of Christ and would have wanted some statements about the nature of Christ's sinlessness that would have stopped all further debate. But we must remember that the New Testament is not a theological treatise; it is about salvation history.[14]

I repeat: We must stand in awe and humility before the greatest miracle of all time. God became man. It has only happened once. And it will never happen again. That is what we must always keep in mind as we discuss the natures of Christ, including the question of His pre-fall or post-fall humanity. No human definitions will suffice and

---

[12] Francis Nichol, ed., *The Seventh-day Adventist Bible Commentary* (Washington, DC: Review and Herald Pub. Assn., 1956), vol. 5, pp. 902, 903.
[13] Henry Liddle and Robert Scott, *Greek-English Lexicon*, vol. 2, p. 1144.
[14] Norman Young, "Jesus—Divinity Revealed in Humanity," in Bryan W. Ball and William G. Johnsson, eds, *The Essential Jesus*, p. 121.

answer all questions. In the end we must humbly confess: We cannot compare Him with anyone else. He is the only One who can save us because, in a miraculous way that far exceeds our understanding, He is both God and man.

# APPENDIX

## Comments of Ellen G. White on Christ's Human Nature

### Christ's Divinity

In Christ is life, original, unborrowed, underived.
*The Desire of Ages*, p. 530

In Christ all fullness dwells. He [Paul] teaches us to count all things but loss for the excellency of the knowledge of Christ Jesus our Lord. This knowledge is the highest science any man can reach. It is the sum of all true science. "This is life eternal," Christ declared, "that they might know thee the only true God, and Jesus Christ, who thou hast sent."
Manuscript 125, 1907; *SDA Bible Commentary*, vol. 7, p. 905

Christ was God essentially, and in the highest sense. He was with God from all eternity, God over all, blessed forevermore. The Lord Jesus Christ, the divine Son of God, existed from eternity, a distinct person, yet one with the Father.
*Selected Messages*, vol. 1, p. 247

### The Incarnation

Laying aside His royal robe and kingly crown, Christ clothed His divinity with humanity, that human beings might be raised from their degradation, and placed on vantage-ground. Christ could not have come to this earth with the glory that He had in the heavenly courts. Sinful human beings could not have borne the sight. He veiled his divinity with the garb of humanity, but He did not part with His divinity. A divine-human Savior, He came to stand at the head of the fallen race, to share in their experience from childhood to manhood.
*The Review and Herald*, June 15, 1905

He [Christ] voluntarily assumed human nature. It was His own act, and by His own consent. He clothed His divinity with humanity. He was all the while as God, but He did not appear as God. He veiled the demonstrations of Deity which had commanded the homage, and called forth the admiration, of the universe of God. He was God while upon the earth, but He divested Himself of the form of God, and in its stead took the form and fashion of a man. He walked the earth as a man.
*The Review and Herald*, July 5, 1887; *SDA Bible Commentary*, vol. 7A, p. (446).

Was the human nature of the Son of Mary changed into the divine nature of the Son of God? No; the two natures were mysteriously blended in one person—the Man Christ Jesus.
*Manuscript Releases*, vol. 21, p. 418

We cannot explain the great mystery of the plan of redemption. Jesus took upon Himself humanity, that He might reach humanity; but we cannot explain how divinity was clothed with humanity.
*The Review and Herald*, Oct. 1, 1889

The Godhead was not made human, and the human was not deified by the blending together of the two natures. Christ did not possess the same sinful, corrupt, fallen disloyalty we possess, for then He could not be a perfect offering.
*Selected Messages*, vol. 3, p. 131

In contemplating the incarnation of Christ in humanity, we stand baffled before an unfathomable mystery, that the human mind can not comprehend.... Divinity and humanity were mysteriously combined, and man and God became one. It is in this union that we find the hope of our fallen race. Looking upon Christ in humanity, we look upon God, and see in Him the brightness of His glory, the express image of His person.
*The Signs of the Times*, July 30, 1896

### Christ's Human Nature
(*see next chapter*)

### Christ's Temptations

Man can never know the strength of the temptations to which the Son of God was subjected. All the temptations that seem so afflicting to man in his daily life, so difficult to resist and overcome, were brought to bear upon Him in as much greater degree as He is superior in His excellence of character to fallen man.
*The Signs of the Times*, August 4, 1887

The divine nature, combined with the human, made Him capable of yielding to Satan's temptations. Here the test to Christ was far greater than that of Adam and Eve, for Christ took our nature, *fallen* but not corrupted, and would not be corrupted unless He received the words of Satan.
*Manuscript Releases*, vol. 16, p. 182

# Chapter 5

# Ellen White and the Human Nature of Jesus Christ

There are countless statements from Ellen White that touch upon the human nature of Christ. A few of these were quoted at the end of the previous chapter. Even if we take into account that many of her statements were "recycled" in later publications and included in various compilations, there is far more material than we can possibly survey in this chapter. Not only is the number of statements a challenge, but also the fact that Ellen White's ministry spans almost seven decades. One may expect that she would express some things in a different way, as her thinking matured over time. Nonetheless, I will try to present a balanced picture of what Ellen White wrote about the human nature of Christ.

Adventists generally believe that analyzing what Ellen White said about the human nature of Christ provides us with many insights that help us to understand the meaning of particular Bible passages. But we should be aware of the fact that her statements often use new terminology and also go beyond what the Bible tells us, as she often adds elements that are not immediately apparent from the biblical material. The value we attach to these special insights depends to a large extent on our view of her inspiration. For some, her writings are mainly of a devotional nature; others (and certainly most Last Generation Theology supporters) believe that she must also play an important role in the formulation of our doctrines, and they tend to give almost equal weight to the Ellen White statements as to the information that we mine from the Bible.

In the previous chapter we saw that not every Bible text about the nature of Christ highlights the same aspects and that we must keep statements with various emphases in balance. And even then we must in all humility accept that much will remain a mystery to our finite minds. When dealing with what Ellen White has said about the human nature of Christ, the challenges do not diminish. Many of her statements can be quoted in support of the pre-fall point of view; i.e., the view that Christ took the kind of human nature that Adam had *before* his "fall" into sin. On the other hand, probably just as many, or maybe even more, statements seem to support the post-fall position; i.e., the conviction that Christ took the kind of human nature that Adam had *after* sin entered the world, including his inherited tendencies or propensities towards sin.

How do we deal with this problem? Is it possible that Ellen White sometimes contradicted herself? Was she always consistent in what she said, or did she perhaps in some instances change her mind? And if so, would that be a major problem for us or can our concept of inspiration accommodate this?

I have chosen a few representative (I think) quotes to illustrate her approach to the human nature of Christ. Rather than quoting a long series of short statements of just one or two sentences, I believe it is better to present a limited number of somewhat longer statements in their immediate context.

### How Christ became man

I will start with a few statements from Mrs. White that do not provide explicit information on whether Christ's human nature was pre-fall or post-fall. The first quote is of particular interest, as Ellen White comments on what it meant that Jesus came in the "form" of a human person:

> Before Christ left Heaven, and came into the world to die, he was taller than any of the angels. He was majestic and lovely. "Who, being in the form of God, thought it not robbery to be equal with God." He took upon himself man's nature. When his ministry commenced, he was but little taller than the common size of men then living upon the earth. Had he come among men with his noble, heavenly form, his outward appearance would have attracted the minds of the people to himself, and he would have been received without the exercise of faith.
>
> About that period Messiah was expected. By many he was looked for to come as a mighty monarch. The Jews had boasted to the Gentiles of his coming, and had dwelt largely upon the great deliverance which he would bring them, that he would reign as king, and put down all authority. Every kingdom and nation would bow to him, and the Jewish nation would reign over them. They had the events of the first and second comings of Christ confounded together.
>
> It was in the order of God that Christ should take upon himself the form and nature of fallen man, that he might be made perfect through suffering, and endure himself the strength of Satan's temptations, that he might the better know

how to succor those who should be tempted. The faith of men in Christ as the Messiah was not to rest in the evidences of sight, and they [were not to] believe on him because of his personal attractions, but because of the excellence of character found in him, which had never been, neither could be found in another.[1]

Another important statement is found in the third volume of *The Spirit of Prophecy*. [The four volumes of the *Spiritual Gifts* series were enlarged to become the *Spirit of Prophecy* series, which formed the basis for her later, more expanded, five-volume *Conflict of the Ages* series, of which *The Desire of Ages* is the third part, followed by *Acts of the Apostles* and *The Great Controversy*.]

The holy angels were horror-stricken that one [Satan] who had been of their number could fall so far as to be capable of such cruelty. Every sentiment of sympathy or pity which they had ever felt for Satan in his exile, was quenched in their hearts. That his envy should be exercised in such a revenge upon an innocent person was enough to strip him of his assumed robe of celestial light, and to reveal the hideous deformity beneath; but to manifest such malignity toward the divine Son of God, who had, with unprecedented self-denial, and love for the creatures formed in his image, come from Heaven and assumed their fallen nature, was such a heinous crime against Heaven that it caused the angels to shudder with horror, and severed forever the last tie of sympathy existing between Satan and the heavenly world.[2]

---
[1] EGW, *Spiritual Gifts*, vol. 4a, p. 115.
[2] EGW, *The Spirit of Prophecy*, vol. 3, p. 183.

From the following quote we deduce that Ellen White does not seem to agree with those who believe that Christ's human nature differed in any respect from ours.

> But many say that Jesus was not like us, that He was not as we are in the world, that He was divine and that we cannot overcome as He overcame. But Paul writes, "Verily, he took not on him the nature of angels; but he took upon him the seed of Abraham. Wherefore in all things it behooved him to be made like unto his brethren."[3]

The next passage I want to quote, which is very pertinent to our topic, is from an article Ellen White wrote in 1871. Similar statements may be found in other many places in her writings. Note that she states that Christ came "in sinful flesh." There is no agreement among Adventist theologians as to what this precisely meant, and whether or not this includes the "sinful propensities" the first couple had after they had sinned.

> This was the reception the Savior met as he came to a fallen world. He left his heavenly home, his majesty, and riches, and high command, and took upon himself man's nature, that he might save the fallen race. Instead of men glorifying God for the honor he had conferred upon them in thus sending his Son in the likeness of sinful flesh, by giving him a place in their affections, there seemed to be no rest nor safety for the infant Savior. Jehovah could not trust to the inhabitants of the world his Son, who came into the world that through his

---
[3] EGW, *Selected Messages*, vol. 3, p. 197.

divine power he might redeem fallen man. He who came to bring life to man, met, from the very ones he came to benefit, insult, hatred, and abuse. God could not trust his beloved Son with men while carrying on his benevolent work for their salvation, and final exaltation to his own throne. He sent angels to attend his Son and preserve his life, till his mission on earth should be accomplished, and he should die by the hands of the very men he came to save.[4]

Ellen White strikes, however, a different tone in a manuscript she wrote two decades later:

[In Christ] the Godhead was not made human, and the human was not deified by the blending together of the two natures. Christ did not possess the same sinful, corrupt, fallen disloyalty we possess, for then He could not be a perfect offering.[5]

The idea that Christ took the kind of humanity that Adam and Eve had after their disobedience and expulsion from paradise is not new. Others have also defended this standpoint. The technical theological term for this view is postlapsarianism (Latin: *post* = after and *lapsus* = fall). Below are a number of Ellen White quotations that, often implicitly, say or suggest that Christ assumed post-fall human nature when He became incarnate.

He was made like unto his brethren, with the same susceptibilities, mental and physical.[6]

---

[4] EGW, "The First Advent of Christ," *The Review and Herald*, Dec. 24, 1872, p. 11.
[5] EGW, MS 94, June 30, 1893.
[6] EGW, "Meetings in Chicago," *The Review and Herald*, Feb. 10, 1885.

In *The Desire of Ages*, one of her most widely read books, Ellen White comments on numerous aspects of Christ's life and ministry. In this book she makes this significant statement:

> It would have been an almost infinite humiliation for the Son of God to take man's nature, even when Adam stood in his innocence in Eden. But Jesus accepted humanity when the race had been weakened by four thousand years of sin. Like every child of Adam He accepted the results of the working of the great law of heredity. What these results were is shown in the history of His earthly ancestors. He came with such a heredity to share our sorrows and temptations, and to give us the example of a sinless life.[7]

What we just read states that when Christ came in human flesh the human race "had been weakened by four thousand years of sin." The next statement seems to be somewhat at odds with what we read in the previous quotation, namely that He "accepted the working of the great law of heredity."

> The offerings presented to the Lord were to be without blemish. These offerings represented Christ, and from this it is evident that Jesus Himself was free from physical deformity. He was the "lamb without blemish and without spot." 1 Peter 1:19. His physical structure was not marred by any defect; His body was strong and healthy.[8]

Christ, the second Adam, came to a world polluted and

---
[7] EGW, *The Desire of Ages*, p. 48.
[8] EGW, *The Desire of Ages*, p. 50.

marred, to live a life of perfect obedience. The race, weakened in moral power, was unable to cope with Satan, who ruled his subjects with cruel authority. Christ came to stand on the field of battle in warfare against all satanic forces. By representing in his life the character of God, he sought to win man back to his allegiance.

Clad in the vestments of humanity, the Son of God came down to the level of those he wished to save. In him was no guile or sinfulness; he was ever pure and undefiled; yet he took upon him our sinful nature. Clothing his divinity with humanity, that he might associate with fallen humanity, he sought to regain for man that which, by disobedience, Adam lost for himself and for the world. In his own character he displayed to the world the character of God.[9]

The following quotation emphasizes that Christ took human nature in "its fallen condition," but on the other hand, the expression "He must pass over the ground where Adam fell," seems to suggest that He started where Adam was *before* the fall.

The Son of God, who is the express image of the Father's person, became man's Advocate and Redeemer. He humbled Himself in taking the nature of man in his fallen condition, but He did not take the taint of sin. As the second Adam He must pass over the ground where Adam fell, meet the wily foe who caused Adam's and Eve's fall, and be tempted in all points as man will be tempted, and overcome every temptation in behalf of man.[10]

---

[9] EGW, "The Importance of Obedience," *The Review and Herald*, Dec. 15, 1896.
[10] EGW, MS 93, 1893.

**Passions and propensities**

Two words that regularly occur in Ellen White's statements on Christ's human nature are the words "passions" and "propensities." However, comparing different passages, it is soon apparent that she did not always use these words in exactly the same way.[11] Here are some examples. Compare the first two quotes with numbers three and four:

> He was a mighty petitioner, not possessing the passions of our human, fallen natures, but compassed with like infirmities, tempted in all points even as we are.[12]

> Not for one moment was there in Him an evil propensity.[13]

> The religion of Jesus Christ we need daily. Everything we do or say comes under the notice of God. We are a spectacle unto the world, to angels, and to men.... The church of Christ is to represent His character.... Though He had all the strength of passion of humanity, never did He yield to temptation to do one single act which was not pure and elevating and ennobling.[14]

> You both need to acquire a habit of self-government, that your thoughts may be brought into subjection to the Spirit of Christ. It is the grace of God that you need in order that your thoughts may be disciplined to flow in the right channel, that

---
[11] See Ralph Larson, *The Word Was Made Flesh*, pp. 22-28.
[12] EGW, *Testimonies for the Church*, vol. 2, p. 508.
[13] EGW, in *The Seventh-day Adventist Bible Commentary*, vol. 5, p. 1128.
[14] EGW, *In Heavenly Places*, p. 155.

the words you utter may be right words, and that your passions and appetites may be subject to the control of reason, and the tongue be bridled against levity and unhallowed censure and faultfinding. "If any man offend not in word, the same is a perfect man, and able also to bridle the whole body." The greatest triumph given us by the religion of Christ is control over ourselves. Our natural propensities must be controlled, or we can never overcome as Christ overcame.[15]

It should not worry us unduly to find that Ellen White apparently used particular terms while giving them different meanings. She noted that this may also be the case in the Bible, since the Bible is given in the language of man and different meanings may be expressed by the same word.[16] Ellen White seems to have used the words "passion" and "propensities" in a more general sense as characteristics that all human being possess, but which may be controlled or eliminated by staying focused on Christ. She often added adjectives such as "corrupt," "lustful," "hateful," "perverted," and others. However, it is clear from such statements as the first two in this section that there were passions and propensities that Christ did not share with ordinary human beings.

Several scholars who have studied Ellen White's use of the word "propensity" have noted that she may have been influenced by the Anglican minister Henry Melvill, one of her favorite authors. In her library was, for instance, a heavily marked copy of the book *Sermons* by Henry Melvill. One of the officials of the Ellen White Estate has analyzed Ellen White's use of the work of Melvill and has concluded that she seems to have agreed with some of Melvill's opinions. It is of

---

[15] EGW, *Testimonies for the Church*, vol. 4, p. 235.
[16] EGW, *Selected Messages*, vol. 1, p. 20.

interest to quote Melvill in this connection:

> But whilst he [Christ] took humanity with the innocent infirmities, he did not take it with the sinful propensities. Here Deity interposed. The Holy Ghost overshadowed the Virgin, and, allowing weakness to be derived from her, forbade wickedness; and so caused that there should be generated a sorrowing and a suffering humanity, but nevertheless an undefiled and spotless; a humanity with tears, but not with stains; accessible to anguish, but not prone to offend; allied most closely with the produced misery but infinitely removed from the producing cause. So that we hold—and give it you as what we believe the orthodox doctrine—that Christ's humanity was not the Adamic humanity, that is, the humanity of Adam before the fall; nor fallen humanity, that is, in every respect the humanity of Adam after the fall. It was not the Adamic, because it had the innocent infirmities of the fallen. It was not the fallen, because it never descended into moral impurity. It was, therefore, most literally our humanity, but without sin.[17]

Melvill believed that before the fall Adam had neither the "innocent infirmities" nor the "sinful propensities" that all humans are born with, and that Christ did accept those "innocent infirmities," such as hunger, thirst, pain, and death, but not the "propensities" towards sin.[18] "Therefore, since Ellen G. White was familiar with these distinctions

---

[17] *Melvill's Sermons*, p. 47, quoted by Denis Fortin in "Ellen White on the Human Nature of Christ," https://www.andrews.edu/~fortind/EGWNatureofChrist.htm.
[18] Tim Poirier, "Sources Clarify Ellen White's Christology," *Ministry*, Dec. 1989, pp. 7-9. George R. Knight, *A Search for Identity*, pp. 123-124.

in Melvill's sermons, it seems reasonable to conclude that she used the expression 'sinful propensities' in a sense similar to that of Melvill."[19]

Another author that Ellen White read and borrowed from, who had a similar understanding of the human nature of Christ, was Octavius Winslow, a prominent evangelical preacher in England. He also argued that Christ did have weaknesses and infirmities but had no corrupt principles in Him. He possessed post-fall infirmities and weaknesses but did not inherit any propensities to sin.[20]

**The Baker Letter**

William Lemuel Henry Baker (1858-1933) was an evangelist, conference administrator, and Bible teacher who served the Seventh-day Adventist church in the United States and Australia.[21] At the time when Baker served in Tasmania as a pastor, Ellen White, who was living in Australia, wrote a long letter to him and his wife. She had taken a keen interest in Baker's spiritual life and in his work. The main part of the letter was an appeal to work more efficiently and to be more fully committed to Christ, but a rather long section in the middle of the letter deals with the topic of the humanity of Christ. Apparently, this was in response to a question Baker had asked. I want to quote the section of the letter that is of special interest to us. It has become an important element in the controversy over the human nature of Christ. The letter was discovered in the mid-1950s and "was a wake-up call to the discussion of Christology."[22] There has been a lot of speculation about the reason for Ellen White's extensive criticism of Baker's inadequate understanding of Christ's human nature. It seems

---

[19] Roy Adams, *The Nature of Christ*, pp. 68-69.
[20] Denis Fortin, "Ellen White on the Human Nature of Christ."
[21] Denis Fortin, "Baker, William Lemuel Henry," in *The Ellen G. White Encyclopedia*, pp. 300-301.
[22] Woodrow Whidden, *Ellen White on the Humanity of Christ*, p. 59.

that Baker's opinions were very much like those of some much more prominent preachers, for instance, A.T. Jones and E.J. Waggoner, but the suggestion that she was, through Baker, also addressing these men has little to commend itself.[23] Here is what she wrote:

> Be careful, exceedingly careful as to how you dwell upon the human nature of Christ. Do not set Him before the people as a man with the propensities of sin. He is the second Adam. The first Adam was created a pure, sinless being, without a taint of sin upon him; he was in the image of God. He could fall, and he did fall through transgressing. Because of sin, his posterity was born with inherent propensities of disobedience. But Jesus Christ was the only begotten Son of God. He took upon Himself human nature, and was tempted in all points as human nature is tempted. He could have sinned; He could have fallen, but not for one moment was there in him an evil propensity. He was assailed with temptations in the wilderness, as Adam was assailed with temptations in Eden.
>
> Brother Baker, avoid every question in relation to the humanity of Christ which is liable to be misunderstood. Truth lies close to the track of presumption. In treating upon the humanity of Christ, you need to guard strenuously every assertion, lest your words be taken to mean more than they imply, and thus you lose or dim the clear perceptions of His humanity as combined with divinity. His birth was a miracle of God; for, said the angel, "Behold, thou shalt conceive in thy womb, and bring forth a son, and shalt call his name JESUS. He shall be great, and shall be called the Son of the Highest: and the

---
[23]*Ibid.*, pp. 60-61.

Lord God shall give unto him the throne of his father David: and he shall reign over the house of Jacob for ever; and of his kingdom there shall be no end. Then said Mary unto the angel, How shall this be, seeing I know not a man? And the angel answered and said to her, The Holy Ghost shall come upon thee, and the power of the Highest shall overshadow thee; therefore also that holy thing which shall be born of thee shall be called the Son of God."

These words do not refer to any human being, except to the Son of the infinite God. Never, in any way, leave the slightest impression upon human minds that a taint of, or inclination to, corruption rested upon Christ, or that He in any way yielded to corruption. He was tempted in all points like as man is tempted, yet He is called "that holy thing". It is a mystery that is left unexplained to mortals that Christ could be tempted in all points like as we are, and yet be without sin. The incarnation of Christ has ever been, and will ever remain a mystery. That which is revealed, is for us and for our children, but let every human being be warned from the ground of making Christ altogether human, such an one as ourselves; for it cannot be. The exact time when humanity blended with divinity, it is not necessary for us to know. We are to keep our feet on the Rock Christ Jesus, as God revealed in humanity.

I perceive that there is danger in approaching subjects which dwell on the humanity of the Son of the Infinite God. He did humble Himself when He saw He was in fashion as a man, that He might understand the force of all temptations wherewith man is beset.[24]

---
[24] EGW, Letter 8, in *The Seventh-day Adventist Bible Commentary*, vol. 5, p. 1128-1129.

One of the key questions with regard to the Baker letter is the precise meaning of the term "propensities"—a matter we have already addressed. With Woodrow Whidden, I believe the most obvious meaning is "natural inclinations to sin."[25]

Having carefully weighed all the evidence, including the content of the Baker letter, Eric Claude Webster concludes

> that Ellen White believed that Christ took upon Himself the nature of man after the fall with all its weaknesses and liabilities, but not with its sin. He stood where every sinner stands in the weakened physical, mental and moral nature, but unlike all sinners, possessing a pure, sinless human nature without the propensities or tendencies to evil.[26]

Woodrow Whidden comes to a similar conclusion, and his summation seems to be a fair description of the state of affairs:

> While the Baker letter has not decisively settled the debate about the nature of Christ, it has played an important role. It has certainly been a compelling statement in support of the so-called pre-Fall position, and the supporters of the post-Fall teaching have struggled with it valiantly. But as the dust is beginning to settle in this lengthy theological debate, it seems that the message of the Baker letter clearly weighs in on the "pre-Fall" side. Its terminology obviously seems to point to a profoundly sinless *uniqueness* in the nature of Christ.[27]

---

[25] Woodrow Whidden, *Ellen White on the Humanity of Christ*, p. 63.
[26] Eric C. Webster, *Crosscurrents in Adventist Christology* (Berrien Springs, MI: Andrews University Press, 1992 edition), p. 133.
[27] Woodrow Whidden, *Ellen White on the Humanity of Christ*, p. 65.

**The sublime uniqueness of Christ**

There is disagreement among Adventist scholars about the right interpretation of what Ellen White wrote about the human nature of Christ. This disagreement is deep-seated and will not easily (if at all) disappear. I strongly believe that we must accept as a fact that Ellen White had no intention to provide us with a complete, systematic Christology. She clearly also struggled to describe the uniqueness of the dual nature of Christ and the kind of humanity He took upon Himself.

What do we take away from reading what she said? All will agree that Ellen White was adamant that Christ was and remained absolutely sinless. There is also no doubt that she wanted to convey to her readers that Christ took humanity to the extent that He could become our Savior, as the one who could fully identify with us and could be our perfect Substitute. The debate about whether or not His humanity included the propensity to sin (or, in more theological language, whether or not He was infected with original sin) is certainly important in the context of our discussion of Last Generation Theology. On the basis of my study I have, with many others, concluded that the pre-fall concept is to be preferred over the post-fall position. But at the same time I realize that we can get so worked up about such issues—important though they might be—that we lose sight of the complete picture. Let us always remember that it is more important that we are *saved* than that we are *right*! Whether we have our theology completely correct or not, we should not be in any doubt that Christ, somehow, became one of us, and forever united divinity with humanity so that we might have eternal life!

"Being found in fashion as a man, He humbled Himself, and

became obedient unto death, even the death of the cross." Phil. 2:8. As the high priest laid aside his gorgeous pontifical robes, and officiated in the white linen dress of the common priest, so Christ took the form of a servant, and offered sacrifice, Himself the priest, Himself the victim. "He was wounded for our transgressions, He was bruised for our iniquities: the chastisement of our peace was upon Him" Isa. 53:5.

Christ was treated as we deserve, that we might be treated as He deserves. He was condemned for our sins, in which He had no share, that we might be justified by His righteousness, in which we had no share. He suffered the death which was ours, that we might receive the life which was His. "With His stripes we are healed."

By His life and His death, Christ has achieved even more than recovery from the ruin wrought through sin. It was Satan's purpose to bring about an eternal separation between God and man; but in Christ we become more closely united to God than if we had never fallen. In taking our nature, the Savior has bound Himself to humanity by a tie that is never to be broken.[28]

When everything is said and done, Christian faith rests upon the glorious fact of "Jesus Christ and him crucified" (1 Corinthians 2:2).[29] Christ became human. He lived and died having assumed, in some way, our human nature. C.S. Lewis hit the nail on the head by saying: "The central Christian belief is that Christ's death has somehow put us right with God and given us a fresh start.... A good many theo-

---
[28]EGW, *The Desire of Ages*, p. 25.
[29]Edward Vick, *Let Me Assure You: Of Grace, of Faith, of Forgiveness, of Freedom, of Fellowship, of Hope* (Mountain View, CA: Pacific Press Pub. Assn., 1968), p. 15.

ries have been held as to how it works; what all Christians are agreed upon is that it *does* work."[30] We have need of a teacher, an example, a revealer and interpreter of God's will. We find all of this in Jesus Christ, "and more, but at the core of this all He is God and Savior."[31]

In whatever ways we stretch our minds to understand what happened when Christ assumed humanity, we will never fully understand the mystery of the incarnation. In 1 Corinthians 1:23 the apostle Paul stated that "a specific person at a specific time and place has significance for all people," but he added that this person had become a "stumbling block" for the Jews and "foolishness" to the Greeks.[32] The only way to avoid falling over this "stumbling block" is in accepting, in all humility, that Christ is our incomparable Savior, who is worthy of our unceasing adoration and our total commitment.

---

[30] C.S. Lewis, *Mere Christianity* (New York: HarperCollins Publishers, 1980 edition), p. 54.
[31] Raoul Dederen, "Christ: His Person and Work," in *Handbook of Seventh-day Adventist Theology*, p. 162.
[32] Van der Kooi and van den Brink, *Christian Dogmatics: An Introduction*, p. 394.

# Chapter 6

# Perfection: Possible or Impossible?

When the character of Christ shall be perfectly reproduced in His people, then He will come to claim them as His own.[1] These few words from the pen of Ellen G. White form perhaps the single most important statement that is used in defense of Last Generation Theology. Here is, it is argued, an inspired assertion that perfection is attainable. In fact, God's people *must* reach a state of character perfection before Christ will return. This raises two important questions: First, does this statement have the clear biblical support the Last Generation Theology believers say it has? And, second, what does Ellen White, in fact, mean when she speaks about perfection? Does she tell us that *sinless* perfection is possible?

This chapter will attempt to answer those two questions and will also touch on a few related issues. As we proceed, I will mention a few statements from Ellen White, but my main argument will be based on the biblical material. In the final section of this chapter I will then, as in some of the previous chapters, present a representative sample of statements from Ellen G. White.

### Perfection and perfectionism in the past

The view that becoming perfect is an attainable goal is not an Adventist invention. Perfectionism is a phenomenon with a very long

---
[1] EGW, *Christ's Object Lessons*, p. 69.

history. Even before Christianity came on the scene we find among the Jewish sect of the Essenes, who lived in the Qumran community near the Dead Sea, clear traces of perfectionism.[2] And throughout the early centuries of Christian history there have been individuals, groups, and even larger movements within the church or at the edges of the church that promoted perfectionism. As history proceeded, from early Christianity into the Middle Ages, members of a wide array of monastic movements forsook "normal" life in order to strive for a state of perfection. We should, however, note the words of a scholar who states that in many cases "the projected 'perfection' was not a state of sinlessness but a mature culmination of the interconnected virtues of humility, self-control, charity and the like."[3]

Closer to our times, perfectionism was an important element of Christian life for such movements as Pietism, Quakerism, and, in particular, Methodism. The Methodist influence on Adventism was, to put it mildly, significant,[4] especially through Ellen White, who came from a Methodist background. The views of Ellen White regarding salvation and sanctification—and also with respect to perfection—resemble in many ways those of John Wesley, the founder of Methodism. We should note that, for Wesley, perfection was not final or absolute. Perfect people, he said, are never so perfect that they are totally sinless. They can always grow more. Jan Barna, a systematician, summarizes Wesley's view in these words: "Wesley's definition of perfec-

---

[2] For a description of perfectionist movements, see H.K. LaRondelle, *Perfection and Perfectionism: A Dogmatic-Ethical Study of Biblical Perfection and Phenomenal Perfectionism* (Kampen, the Netherlands: J.H. Kok NV, 1971), pp. 246-324. Also: R. Newton Flew, *The Idea of Perfection in Christian Theology* (Eugene, OR: Wipf and Stock, 2005 edition).
[3] Paul M. Blowers, "Perfectionism," in *New Westminster Dictionary of Church History* (Louisville, KY: Westminster John Knox Press, 2008), p. 508.
[4] See Jan Barna, *Adventism and Biblical Perfection: The Diverse Roots of Perfectionist Thinking in Adventism and the Need for Biblical Definition of Perfection* (paper presented during the Bible Symposium on Perfectionism: Adventism and Biblical Perfection, South England Conference, Feb. 5, 2013).

tion is at its core internal love of God that rules the entire life." [5]

Another perfectionist influence on Adventism came from the Keswick Movement and other holinesss movements in the late 19th century.[6] The term "holiness movements" covers a wide array of groups (and eventually denominations), with mostly Methodist roots, that emphasized the "holiness" requirement and often stressed perfection as a central belief. The Keswick Movement, also called the Higher Life Movement, which was heavily influenced by the teachings of Wesley, exerted a major influence on the thinking of A.T. Jones in the later phase of his life. Jones played a dominant role in the 1888 General Conference in Minneapolis, but he eventually deviated from mainstream Adventist theology.

"Essentially, Keswick theology teaches that the Christian life consists of two primary crises (or major turning points): justification and sanctification, both of which happen at *different* times in the life of the believer. After salvation one must have *another* encounter with the Spirit; otherwise, he or she will not progress into holiness or the 'deeper' things of God." Some Keswick teachers would say that sinless perfection is possible after one has had this deeper encounter with the Spirit, also often referred to as the "second blessing."[7]

**Some relevant Adventist experiences**

The concept of Christian perfection is usually related to a careful adherence to the divine instructions that are revealed in the Bible. Often this will lead to a form of legalism, where salvation is no longer primarily the result of God's free grace but, at least in part, the reward for human obedience to God's laws. Early Adventism continuously

---
[5] *Ibid.*, p. 3.
[6] *Ibid.*, pp. 5-8.
[7] www.gotquestions.org/Keswick-movement.html.

struggled with the tendency to place a one-sided emphasis on obedience to God's commandments, the Sabbath commandment in particular. This was perhaps to be expected as the Adventist believers were constantly forced to defend their Sabbath practice. However, the sad reality was that, as a result, the basic Christian truth that salvation is by grace, through faith in Jesus Christ, was often seriously obscured. This led Ellen White to an oft-quoted and rather strong statement: "We have preached the law until we are as dry as the hills of Gilboa that had neither dew or rain."[8] The issue came to a climax during the 1888 General Conference in the city of Minneapolis, where A.T. Jones and E.J. Waggoner (with the support of Ellen G. White) soon dominated the proceedings with their powerful messages on righteousness by faith.[9] Their presentations met with stiff opposition during those historic meetings from (mostly older) church leaders. In retrospect we can see that the conference was a turning point in the Adventist struggle against the legalism that emphasized human works, in favor of a gospel emphasis on Christ's work on our behalf. Even today Adventism all too often strays towards a legalistic concept of the Christian life.

Around the year 1900 Adventism experienced a serious crisis with the emergence of the "Holy Flesh Movement."[10] The center of the short-lived movement was in the American state of Indiana. Its appearance shows that Adventism was not isolated from the general religious climate, which at that time saw dozens of groups and per-

---

[8] *The Ellen G. White 1888 Materials*, p. 560. See https://text.egwwritings.org/publication.php?pubtype=Book&bookCode=1888&pagenumber=560.
[9] Many books have been written on the 1888 Minneapolis Conference about its main players and the issues at stake, as well as about the aftermath. For a concise guide to the topic, see George R. Knight, *A User-Friendly Guide to the 1888 Message* (Hagerstown, MD: Review and Herald Pub. Assn., 1998).
[10] See Lowell Tarling, *The Edges of Seventh-day Adventism* (Barragga Bay, Australia: Galilee Publishing, 1981), pp. 74-83; Gary Land, "Holy Flesh Movement," in Denis Fortin and Jerry Moon, eds., *The Ellen G. White Encyclopedia*, pp. 873-874.

sonalities in various branches of evangelical Christianity being affected by the holiness movement, to which I referred in the previous paragraphs. Albion Fox Ballenger (1861-1921), a popular Adventist revival preacher who emphasized the crucial role of the Holy Spirit in Christian thought and life, provided much of the theological basis on which others built in a more radical fashion.[11] The leaders of the Holy Flesh Movement, which was characterized by a high pitch of excitement and all kinds of physical demonstrations, insisted that the true followers of Christ must pass through a "Garden of Gethsemane experience." They taught that true conversion replaces "corruptible earthly flesh—an experience similar to what Christ went through in the Garden of Gethsemane. Believers who would be alive at Christ's second coming must have gone through that experience. Ellen White, who at the time had just returned to the United States from her nine-year stay in Australia, played an important role in discouraging a further spread of the movement. During the General Conference Session in April 1901 she insisted that human beings cannot receive holy flesh prior to the second coming and that the teachings of this movement not only led to fanaticism and confusion but would inevitably also lead to the conclusion that the truly converted would be perfect. In addition, she warned her audience that it would give birth to the further idea that everything they did would also be holy![12]

Another wave of commotion within Adventism about character development and perfection centered around the activities of Robert Brinsmead (b. 1933) and his followers. Robert—with the support of his brother John—came into sharp conflict with the church in Australia. His theological journey took different twists and turns,

---

[11] Calvin W. Edwards and Gary Land, *Seeker after Light: A.F. Ballenger, Adventism, and American Christianity* (Berrien Springs, MI: Andrews University Press, 2000), pp. 32-64.
[12] Fortin and Moon, *The Ellen G. White Encyclopedia*, p. 874.

and later in life he promoted views that were totally opposite to what he had preached and written in the 1960s and 1970s. In that period Brinsmead advocated a form of perfectionism that he described as the "Sanctuary Awakening Message." While the true believers would undergo a *physical* transformation at Christ's second coming, a *spiritual* transformation was to take place prior to that through a special outpouring of the Holy Spirit, which would "perfect and seal" the believers and enable them to live sinlessly, after the close of probation, without the need of a Mediator.[13] At some point he concluded that even sinful thoughts and emotions would be miraculously erased. In many respects several of Brinsmead's ideas during this period of his life resemble the main features of Last Generation Theology.[14]

**The Bible on perfection**

It is important to understand that issues surrounding legalism and perfectionism have occupied Christians through the ages, including—as has been shown in the previous section—Seventh-day Adventist Christians. Adventist theologians, church leaders, and members in the pew have often argued in the past that sinless perfection can be attained. Others have vehemently rejected that position. In 1975 the Southern Publishing Association (a rather innovative Adventist publishing firm that was forced to merge with the Review and Herald Publishing Association in 1980) published a unique book in which four Adventist theologians explained their diverging views regarding perfection. It is interesting to see this open dialogue between proponents of the pro- and anti-position—something we have not often

---

[13] https://en.wikipedia.org/wiki/Robert_Brinsmead; see also Geoffrey J. Paxton, *The Shaking of Adventism* (Grand Rapids, MI: Baker Book House, 1978 ed.), pp. 96-103.
[14] Richard W. Schwarz and Floyd Greenleaf, *Light Bearers: A History of the Seventh-day Adventist Church* (Nampa, ID: Pacific Press Pub. Assn., 1995), pp. 623-625.

seen since![15] The contribution of Hans K. Larondelle is perhaps the most helpful in determining what is the biblical view of perfection.[16] It is a condensed version of his highly praised PhD dissertation.[17] And indeed, the Bible must decide the issue for us.

In His Sermon on the Mount, Jesus challenged His audience: "Be ye therefore perfect, even as your Father which is in heaven is perfect" (Matthew 5:48, KJV). Writing to the Ephesians about the unity and the diverse ministries in the church, the apostle Paul explained:

> And he gave some, apostles; and some, prophets; and some, evangelists; and some, pastors and teachers; for the perfecting of the saints…till we all come in the unity of the faith, and of the knowledge of the Son of God, unto a perfect man, unto the measure of the stature of the fullness of Christ (Ephesians 4:11-13, KJV).

I quoted these few verses from the King James Version, since most recent Bible translations do not use the terms "perfect" or "perfection," but speak of "mature" and "maturity." We find a similar use of perfection versus maturity in the KJV and other translations of Hebrews 6:1. In the NIV, the author admonishes the believers to "move beyond the elementary teachings" and progress "to maturity" (KJV: "unto perfection").

A number of times the Old Testament refers to persons who were "perfect." Noah is one of them. Here again, the word "perfect" is found in the KJV, but is avoided by newer versions. We read in the KJV that

---

[15] Herbert E. Douglas, Edward Heppenstall, Hans K. LaRondelle, and C. Mervyn Maxwell, *Perfection: The Impossible Possibility* (Nashville, TN: Southern Pub. Assn., 1975).
[16] Hans K. LaRondelle, "Biblical Idea of Perfection," in *Perfection: The Impossible Possibility*, pp. 93-136.
[17] Hans K. LaRondelle, *Perfection and Perfectionism: A Dogmatic-Ethical Study of Biblical Perfection and Phenomenal Perfectionism*.

Noah "was a just man and perfect in his generations" (Genesis 6:9). The NIV describes Noah as "a righteous man, blameless among the people of his time." The KJV rendering should immediately set some bells ringing. Was Noah a perfect man? What about the incident after the Flood when we find this so-called perfect man in a state of drunkenness in his tent? Or to take another example: In Genesis 17:1 God challenges Abraham to be "perfect" (KJV) or "blameless" (NIV). Anyone who has some knowledge of the Bible would not describe Abraham as a faultless person. Quite clearly he did not reach a state of sinlessness! Job is characterized as "blameless and upright" (NIV). Here also the KJV tells us that this patriarch was "perfect" (Job 1:1).

A number of biblical passages clearly underline that "perfection" is not some vague desire, or a beautiful but impossible ideal, but a requirement for all believers. *The issue is, therefore, not whether perfection is possible, but what is meant by perfection.*[18]

The Greek word for perfection (*teleios*) has the same basic connotation as the Hebrew words *tāmîn* and *salêm*. Language experts agree that these words do not refer to absolute sinlessness. The word *teleios*, we read in *The New International Dictionary of New Testament Theology*, is based on the word *telos*, meaning "end" or "goal." It may refer to the end of time—not as a sudden, abrupt end but as the conclusion of a dynamic process. But *teleios* more often points to "that which has reached its goal, and is thus completed and perfected."[19] In the fullest sense it can only be applied to God (Matthew 5:48) and to Jesus Christ (Hebrews 7:28). The concept of *teleios*, the author of the article in this prestigious dictionary insists, does not carry the idea of ethical perfection that is to be gradually acquired. It refers to a state

---
[18] George R. Knight, *Sin and Salvation*, p. 138.
[19] R. Schippers, "Goal," in Colin Brown, ed., *The New International Dictionary of New Testament Theology*, (Exeter, GB: The Paternoster Press, 1976) vol. 2, pp. 59-65.

of maturity, of having come of age. It does not denote some endpoint of human conduct, but rather the "undivided wholeness of a person in his behavior."[20]

Richard Rice, a prominent Adventist theologian, makes the same kind of comment. Perfection, he says, has to do with the process that leads to the goal of spiritual maturity, and a person may be "perfect" in each stage of development. The aim is to stay on course! A person who is "perfect" in the New Testament sense of the word has not reached a state of sinlessness. The focus must be on attitude rather than on behavior.[21] Says Marvin Moore, a prolific conservative Adventist author, "Perfection is more a state of being, more a relationship with Jesus, more a way of life than it is a 'point' one can measure or know when he has reached it."[22]

Ivan Blazen, a theology professor-emeritus, agrees with this assessment. Biblical perfection means: maturity, wholeness, commitment, full dedication.[23] When the Bible speaks of people like Noah, Abraham, and Job as perfect or blameless, we meet some immediate qualifiers like "walking with God," "fearing God," or "turning from evil." The perfect must find their way in life through their righteousness (according to the KJV of Proverbs 11:5). The New Living Translation puts this in clearer language: "The godly are directed by honesty." They have not achieved perfection in the sense of being sinless, but they aim for it and the right attitude will help them to stay on course. In his prayer of dedication for the temple, King Solomon expressed this attitude in these sublime words: "And may your hearts be fully committed to the Lord our God, to live by his decrees and obey his

---

[20] *Ibid.*, p. 65.
[21] Richard Rice, *The Reign of God,* pp. 280-282.
[22] Marvin Moore, *The Refiner's Fire* (Nampa, ID: Pacific Press Pub. Assn., 2014), p. 114.
[23] Ivan Blazen, "Salvation," in Raoul Dederen, ed., *Handbook of Seventh-day Adventist Theology*, pp. 298-300.

commands" (1 Kings 8:61, NIV). This is what the King James Version means when it uses the term "perfect" in the same verse: "Let your heart therefore be perfect with the Lord our God."

**Love: the center of biblical perfection**

Let us take another look at Matthew 5:48 and compare this verse with its parallel in the Gospel of Luke. Instead of echoing the very same words ("be perfect"), Luke reports Jesus' words as "Be merciful, just as your Father is merciful" (Luke 6:36). *Could it be that the essence of biblical perfection is found in receiving and giving love?* When we read Matthew 5:48 in its wider context, we notice how the word "love" is mentioned a number of times. That we are sons and daughters of God is demonstrated in our love for others, even for those who are our enemies. Loving others is the distinguishing mark of God's children. After all, did God not already love us before we loved Him? "Therefore," Matthew 5:48 says, we must be perfect in love and reflect the Fatherly love of God.

Reading the first letter of John, we get the distinct impression that love is the essence of our spiritual pilgrimage. According to Paul, it even surpasses faith and hope (1 Corinthians 13:13). Christ's ideal for us is that we shall be "perfect in love" (1 John 4:18). "This is love: not that we loved God, but that he loved us and sent his Son as an atoning sacrifice for our sins. Dear friends, since God so loved us, we also ought to love one another. No one has ever seen God; but if we love one another, God lives in us and his love is made complete in us.... God is love. Whoever lives in love, lives in God and God in them. In this way love is made complete in us so that we will have confidence on the day of judgment: In this world we are like Jesus" (1 John 4:10-17). The apostle Paul stresses the same point: "The only thing that counts is faith expressing itself through love" (Galatians 5:6).

The story of the rich young man that is told in Matthew 19:16-30 is also relevant in this connection. This man came to Jesus and asked, "Teacher, what good thing must I do to get eternal life?" The answer is: "If you want to enter life, obey the commandments." At the man's request Jesus then becomes more specific and lists a few of the Ten Commandments. The young man replies that he has kept all these commandments faithfully. And he adds: "What do I still lack?" Then Jesus answered, "If you want to be *perfect*, go, sell your possessions and give to the poor, and you will have treasure in heaven. Then come, follow me." Being "perfect," it is clear, is not a matter of outward compliance to a series of instructions—important though they may be—but requires a consistent attitude of love as the basis for reaching our spiritual goal.

*Love is the key to biblical perfection.* The passage of 1 Thessalonians 3:12-13 makes this abundantly clear. Paul expressed his hope for the believers in Thessalonica in these powerful words: "May the Lord make your love increase and overflow for each other and for everyone else, just as ours does for you. May he strengthen your hearts so that you will be blameless and holy in the presence of our God and Father when our Lord Jesus comes with all his holy ones." And he ends this letter with these words: "May God himself, the God of peace, sanctify you through and through. May your whole spirit, soul and body be kept blameless at the coming of our Lord Jesus Christ" (1 Thessalonians 5:23).

I believe this adequately clarifies the biblical meaning of perfection or blamelessness. But what about the quotation in Ellen White's book *Christ's Object Lessons* that was cited at the beginning of this chapter? At the end of this section it seems good to repeat this quote, but now with a bit more context. We find this oft-quoted statement in the chapter that provides a commentary on the parable of the sower. It is about the person who sows, but especially about the seed that is sown, its germination, and its gradual growth. What follows is probably the longest quote from Ellen White that you will find in this book. Read it carefully, and then decide whether the few words from this section, which are so often detached from their context, are in reality such a strong basis for the premise of Last Generation Theology, that there will eventually be a group of people who have reached the point of sinless perfection!

> The germination of the seed represents the beginning of spiritual life, and the development of the plant is a beautiful figure of Christian growth. As in nature, so in grace; there can be no life without growth. The plant must either grow or die. As its growth is silent and imperceptible, but continuous, so is the development of the Christian life. *At every stage of development our life may be perfect; yet if God's purpose for us is fulfilled, there will be continual advancement.* Sanctification is the work of a lifetime. As our opportunities multiply, our experience will enlarge, and our knowledge increase. We shall become strong to bear responsibility, and our maturity will be in proportion to our privileges....
>
> So the Christian is to grow by co-operating with the divine agencies. Feeling our helplessness, we are to improve all the opportunities granted us to gain a fuller experience. As the plant takes root in the soil, so we are to take deep root in Christ. As the plant receives the sunshine, the dew, and the

rain, we are to open our hearts to the Holy Spirit. The work is to be done "not by might, nor by power, but by My Spirit, saith the Lord of hosts." Zech. 4:6. If we keep our minds stayed upon Christ, He will come unto us "as the rain, as the latter and former rain unto the earth." Hosea 6:3. As the Sun of Righteousness, He will arise upon us "with healing in His wings." Mal. 4:2. We shall "grow as the lily." We shall "revive as the corn, and grow as the vine." Hosea 14:5, 7. By constantly relying upon Christ as our personal Savior, we shall grow up into Him in all things who is our head....

There can be no growth or fruitfulness in the life that is centered in self. If you have accepted Christ as a personal Saviour, you are to forget yourself, and try to help others. *Talk of the love of Christ*, tell of His goodness. Do every duty that presents itself. Carry the burden of souls upon your heart, and by every means in your power seek to save the lost. As you receive the Spirit of Christ—*the Spirit of unselfish love and labor for others*—you will grow and bring forth fruit. The graces of the Spirit will ripen in your character. *Your faith will increase, your convictions deepen, your love be made perfect. More and more you will reflect the likeness of Christ in all that is pure, noble, and lovely.*

"The fruit of the Spirit is love, joy, peace, longsuffering, gentleness, goodness, faith, meekness, temperance." Gal. 5:22, 23. This fruit can never perish, but will produce after its kind a harvest unto eternal life. "When the fruit is brought forth, immediately he putteth in the sickle, because the harvest is come." Christ is waiting with longing desire for the manifestation of Himself in His church. When the character of Christ shall be perfectly reproduced in His people, then He will come to claim them as His own.

It is the privilege of every Christian not only to look for but to hasten the coming of our Lord Jesus Christ, (2 Peter 3:12, margin). Were all who profess His name bearing fruit to His glory, how quickly the whole world would be sown with the seed of the gospel. Quickly the last great harvest would be ripened, and Christ would come to gather the precious grain.[24]

**Sinlessness**

Can we live without sinning? Some biblical passages seem to suggest that it is possible. Says 1 John 3:6: "No one who lives in him [Christ] keeps on sinning. No one who continues to sin has either seen him or known him." And verse 9: "No one who is born of God will continue to sin, because God's seed remains in them; they cannot go on sinning, because they have been born of God." The same thought is repeated in 1 John 5:18: "We know that anyone born of God does not continue to sin."

However, in the same short letter from John we also read something that sounds very different. In fact, it seems to be in direct contradiction with the verses just quoted. 1 John 1:8-10 states unequivocally: "If we claim to be without sin, we deceive ourselves and the truth is not in us.... If we claim we have not sinned, we make him [Christ] out to be a liar and his word is not in us."

How can we reconcile these seemingly contradictory statements? Romans 6 can help us here. Paul argues that those who have accepted Christ have "died to sin" (verses 2, 11) and "have been set

---

[24]EGW, *Christ's Object Lessons*, pp. 65-69; italics supplied.

free from sin" (verse 22). This means, the apostle says, that sin no longer "reigns" in us and that we are no longer slaves to sin but slaves of God (verses 12, 18, 22). Paul was a man of great faith but also a man who was painfully aware of his sinfulness. He never reached sinless perfection. In his "inner being" he delights in God's law, and he has "the desire to do what is good," but he finds that he continues to commit sins, however much he tries not to. "Although I want to do good, evil is right there with me." This realization brings him to the point of despair and he cries out: "What a wretched man I am!" (Romans 7:18-24).

In his letter to the Philippians Paul tells the addressees, whom he describes as "mature" ("perfect," KJV), about the dynamic process that continues to define his own life as a follower of Christ: "Not that I have already obtained all this, or have already been made perfect, but I press on to take hold of that for which Christ Jesus took hold of me. Brothers, I do not consider myself yet to have taken hold of it. But one thing I do: Forgetting what is behind and straining toward what is ahead, I press on toward the goal to win the prize for which God has called me heavenward in Christ Jesus" (Philippians 3:12-15, NIV, 1978).

"Mature" believers no longer have sin as the governing principle in their lives; they are *teleios* (perfect) because they have a clear *telos* (goal). It is one of the great paradoxes of faith that believers can be called perfect (mature) even though they must still grow further. They do still commit sins, for which they continue to need forgiveness, and they are still subject to sins of omission and subconscious wrongdoings. (Remember what we said about the nature of sin in chapter 3.) They are not sinless in any absolute sense of the word, but they have ceased to be slaves of sin! They were justified when they accepted

Christ, and they are being sanctified as they live the life of a disciple of Christ. Let us not forget that both justification and sanctification are 100 percent the work of God. "Genuine sanctification—let it be repeated—stands or falls with this continued orientation toward justification and the remission of sin."[25] "Now that you have been set free from sin and have become slaves of God, the benefit you reap leads to holiness, and the result is eternal life. For the wages of sin is death, but the gift of God is eternal life in Christ Jesus our Lord" (Romans 6:22-23).

Ivan Blazen has summarized what we have discussed in this section in these two succinct statements:

> Paradoxically, perfection as present is sanctification; sanctification as future is perfection. This means that the two realities are part and parcel of the same reality—likeness to God.[26]

And

> Perfection is not so much something we reach, as something that reaches us, not so much as what we attain, as something which grasps our life from beyond.[27]

**Legalism**

Unfortunately, the concept of biblical perfection has all too often been dominated by negative overtones. The emphasis is frequently so much on what Christ must do *in* us, that what Christ has done

---
[25] G.C. Berkouwer, *Studies in Dogmatics: Faith and Sanctification* (Grand Rapids, MI: William. B. Eerdmans Publishing Company, 1952), p. 87.
[26] Ivan Blazen, "Salvation," in *Handbook of Seventh-day Adventist Theology*, p. 299.
[27] *Ibid.*, p. 300.

*for* us has been largely obscured.[28] For many who believe that they should strive for perfection and that a state of sinless perfection is, in fact, possible, the Christian life is mostly a matter of fighting against, and overcoming, the many things they believe they should no longer do. Many have been caught in the deadly net of legalism; that is, in a constant effort to conform to a long list of rules and regulations.

In Old Testament times meticulous adherence to the Mosaic laws had often given Israel a false sense of security—as if following a strict ritualistic program would automatically guarantee a right relationship with God. The prophet Micah does not mince words in this clear message for his people:

> With what shall I come before the Lord
> and bow down before the exalted God?
> Shall I come before him with burnt offerings,
> with calves a year old?
> Will the Lord be pleased with thousands of rams,
> with ten thousand rivers of olive oil?
> Shall I offer my firstborn for my transgression,
> the fruit of my body for the sin of my soul?
> He has shown you, O mortal, what is good.
> And what does the Lord require of you?
> To act justly and to love mercy
> and to walk humbly with your God (Micah 6:6-8).

The proverbial culprits (and, actually, also victims) of legalism were the scribes and Pharisees we meet in the Gospel narratives. They had carefully studied Moses' laws and had tacked on many fur-

---
[28] Richard Rice, *The Reign of God*, p. 281.

ther regulations to the 613 commandments they felt could be distilled from the Torah. They tried to be "perfect" in their adherence to all these rules. But were they commended by Jesus for their "perfect" keeping of the law? The Lord told them straight to their faces that in all their religious zeal and relentless striving for perfection they had sadly forgotten what was much more important: justice, mercy, and faithfulness (Matthew 23:23).

Seventh-day Adventism has had (and still has) more than its share of legalists. In their tireless efforts to be acceptable in God's sight, these legalists want to be obedient to all His commandments—to all the rules they find in the Bible and, usually, also to the many instructions they believe God has given His church through the ministry of Ellen G. White. More often than not their special focus is on the minutiae of Sabbath keeping and on matters of diet, jewelry, tithing, fashion, music, etc. And also, more often than not, the list tends to become ever longer and more detailed! But do these outward actions define Christian discipleship? The popular Christian author Philip Yancey writes in his marvelous book *What's So Amazing About Grace?*:

> The church I grew up in had much to say about hairstyle, jewelry, and rock music, but not a word about racial injustice and the plight of blacks in the South. In Bible College, not once did I hear a reference to the Holocaust in Germany, perhaps the most heinous sin in all history. We were too busy measuring skirts to worry about such contemporary political issues as nuclear war, racism, or world hunger.[29]

---
[29] Philip Yancey, *What's So Amazing About Grace?* (Grand Rapids, MI: Zondervan Publishing House, 1997), pp. 200-201.

A legalistic striving for perfection is wrong and dangerous for a number of important reasons:

- *Legalists tend to have an inadequate view of sin.* For them sin is primarily a matter of outward behavior. Overcoming sin equals doing or no longer performing certain actions. However, legalists often fail to see that sin is much more than following a detailed set of rules. And, therefore, legalism will never be a road to sinlessness. (See chapter 3.) Legalism easily creates the deceptive sense that one is making real progress and that the goal of sinlessness is in sight.
- *In Romans 6 Paul defines the Christian life as no longer being a slave of sin but being a slave of Christ.* In other words, the Lordship of Christ is the center. Knowing and accepting Christ as our Lord will determine the direction of our lives. Being totally focused on a long list of dos and don'ts puts our own ego in the spotlight. Legalism leads towards an unhealthy preoccupation with ourselves.[30] In extreme cases this preoccupation with oneself can be literally deadly. I was struck (and embarrassed) by a statement of Philip Yancey in his book about grace, in which he discussed legalism. He reported that a friend of his had to preach a funeral service for a young Seventh-day Adventist who had starved himself to death out of concern over which foods were permissible to eat.[31]
- *Jesus warned His followers not to imitate the Pharisees.* He could not have been clearer than when He addressed them as "you hypocrites." By its very nature, Yancey says, "legalism encourages hypocrisy because it defines a set of behavior that may cloak what is going on inside.... The emphasis on externals

---
[30] Richard Rice, *The Reign of God*, p. 281.
[31] Philip Yancey, *What's So Amazing About Grace?*, p. 199.

makes it easy for a person to fake it, to conform, even while suppressing, or hiding, inner problems."[32] There are simply too many examples of deplorable hypocrisy in Christianity to ignore this danger of legalism. "The tendency to hide real sins under a cloak of piety, abstaining from things that are never prohibited in Scripture, and following practices that are never commanded, is as evident in the history of Protestantism as elsewhere."[33] And, I am sorry to add, also in the history of Adventism.

- *Legalists are selective in their list of dos and don'ts.* It may be that those who are caught in legalism will strongly deny this, but when we observe them over time this seems invariably to be the case. The inevitability of our selectivity in literally following biblical instructions is described in an insightful (and often quite humorous) book by a New York journalist who decided to spend a year of his life as "the year of living biblically." For over 12 months he made it his full-time job to abide by all the dos and don'ts (more than 700) that he had found in Scripture. He discovered that it simply could not be done and that he had to be selective.[34]

- *Legalism makes one judgmental.* A constant measuring of one's own progress on the road towards perfection leads to applying the same measuring stick to the behavior of others. Legalists will see it as their duty to warn others to stop their allegedly sinful acts. They tend to forget that God has reserved the judgment for Himself. Legalists fail to understand adequately that

---
[32]*Ibid.*, p. 203.
[33]Michael Horton, *The Christian Faith: A Systematic Theology for Pilgrims on the Way* (Grand Rapids, MI: Zondervan, 2011), p. 666.
[34]A. J. Jacobs, *The Year of Living Biblically: One Man's Humble Quest to Follow the Bible as Literally as Possible* (New York: Simon and Schuster, 2007).

the road towards Christian maturity is living a loving life, demonstrating by performing loving actions that one has become a "slave" of Christ.
- *The Christian life should be characterized by joy, but in many cases the life of a legalist is burdened by endless frustration.* Instead of enjoying the freedom that is anchored in the grace of Christ, many legalists suffer from a sense of persistent failure. It seems there are ever more challenges to confront, new temptations to overcome, and new shortcomings to remedy. Many legalists see their religious journey stranded in total disillusion. Early in his life as a monk, Martin Luther, the great Reformer, racked his brain as long as six hours a day in a frantic effort to remember the sins he might have committed the previous day! The joy in Christ only came later when he had discovered righteousness by faith and exchanged that for his legalistic past. The true Christian, who has accepted the Lordship of Christ and is no longer a slave to sin, will realize that he or she is still far from perfect, in the sense of being sinless. The solution to sin is not to impose an ever-stricter code of behavior. The solution is to "grow in the grace and knowledge of our Lord and Savior Jesus Christ" (2 Peter 3:18).

*When all is said and done, perfectionism is really a moot point!* Richard Rice asks the poignant question: Have you ever seen anyone who has already attained a state of sinless perfection? And then he adds: "A truly sinless person would not even be aware of the fact."[35]

## Ellen White on perfection

The statements by Ellen White on perfection and perfectionism

---
[35] Richard Rice, *The Reign of God*, p. 282.

and related topics (such as sinlessness) are too numerous to list in the context of this book. There is a never-ending series of compilations of these statements. Usually the bias of the compiler is clearly visible.[36] [I hope you will find no such bias in the Appendix to this chapter.] The problem is that Ellen White has made different kinds of statements with regard to the issue of perfection. There are many instances where she describes perfection as a divine standard and an obligation to be fulfilled, but other statements clearly suggest that total sinlessness is not within human reach. She often employs the language of possibility, using words such as "may" or "can." And in many of her statements she points to constant growth and development in living a life that is graced by love.

In the Appendix to this chapter you will find a number of statements that fall in either category. In some statements Ellen White appears to say that sinlessness is possible, while she flatly denies this in other statements. The dilemma is quite similar to what we encountered when looking at the relevant Bible passages (in particular in 1 John). And the solution is also quite similar. The bottom line is: *True believers are no longer under the dominion of sin*, even though they will not be fully sinless until the second coming of Jesus Christ. They may be perfect in the sense of being "mature" while they continue to grow in grace towards the final goal of perfection.

Several Adventist scholars have carefully analyzed what Ellen White has said about sinlessness and perfection and have concluded that her views (and her use of language) on this issue very much resembles that of the great Methodist leader and theologian John Wesley.[37] He made a distinction between sin as a way of life and

---

[36] A very helpful article by Richard Rice is "Sanctification and Perfection: Another Look," *Ministry*, June 1984, pp. 6-8, 15.
[37] See the PhD dissertation by Woodrow W. Whidden, *The Soteriology of Ellen G White: The Persistent Path*

occasional mistakes, using the words "proper" and "improper" sins, and differentiating between perfection of direction and perfection of action. For Wesley, perfection is not a state of sinlessness, as these words plainly indicate: *By perfection I mean the humble, gentle, patient love of God, and our neighbour, ruling our tempers, words, and actions. I do not include an impossibility of falling from it, either in part or in whole.*[38]

In any case, the statements of Ellen G. White must be read within the biblical framework. They do not lay the foundation on which we may try to construct a theory with the biblical passages as building blocks. The Bible must inform our reading of Ellen White and not vice versa! If we follow that course we will discover that she made it very clear that *God's forgiving grace runs side by side with His empowering grace.*[39]

Richard Rice concludes an article in *Ministry* (the journal for Adventist clergy) as follows, and we do well to keep these words in mind:

> We see, then, that Ellen White's statements affirming the possibility of perfection serve the purpose of encouragement, rather than prediction. They refer to an ideal that gives direction and motivation to the Christian's experience rather than to a specific level of achievement that will actually be reached at some point during this life.[40]

Time and time again Ellen White challenges her readers to reproduce the character of Christ, but she also reminds them that they will

---

*to Perfection, 1836-1902* (Drew University, 1989).
[38]http://www.ccel.org/ccel/wesley/perfection.ii.vi.html. See also John Wesley's book *A Plain Account of Christian Perfection* (London: Epsworth, 1952).
[39]George R. Knight, *Sin and Salvation*, p. 159.
[40]Richard Rice, "Sanctification and Perfection," p. 8.

never equal it.[41] Note these important words:

> Ministers especially should know the character and works of Christ, that they may imitate Him; for the character and works of a true Christian are like His. He laid aside His glory, His dominion, His riches, and sought after those who were perishing in sin. He humbled Himself to our necessities, that He might exalt us to heaven. Sacrifice, self-denial, and disinterested benevolence characterized His life. He is our pattern. Have you, Brother A, imitated the Pattern? I answer: No. He is a perfect and holy example, given for us to imitate. *We cannot equal the pattern*; but we shall not be approved of God if we do not copy it and, *according to the ability which God has given, resemble it*. Love for souls for whom Christ died will lead to a denial of self and a willingness to make any sacrifice in order to be co-workers with Christ in the salvation of souls.[42]

**God's vindication**

Before we end this chapter there is one final issue that must be briefly mentioned. Last Generation Theology supporters tell us that the presence of a perfect final generation is so important because it is a unique demonstration to the universe that God has been fair all along in demanding that His law be kept. Satan had, so it is argued, maintained that it was impossible for human beings to do what God asked them to do. God was unreasonable and this meant that His divine reputation was at stake before the entire universe. According to Last Generation Theology supporters, the perfect final generation at long last demonstrates that God's law can be kept. This vindicates God, seals the final defeat of Satan, and brings the conflict between

---
[41] George R. Knight, *Sin and Salvation*, p. 160.
[42] EGW, *Testimonies for the Church*, vol. 2, p. 549; italics supplied.

good and evil to a final close.

Where is the biblical evidence for this view? I cannot find any. And neither does there appear to be any basis for this in the writings of Ellen G. White. There is not the "faintest suggestion" nor "the slightest hint" in her writings, Marvin Moore concludes after having made a careful study of this matter, "that God is waiting on them [i.e., the final perfect generation] to accomplish anything to bring the plan of salvation or the great controversy to a close." Jesus is the One who vindicated God and defeated Satan 2,000 years ago. He is the "only One who could have accomplished that, and once He did it, there is nothing left for any other generation to do."[43]

**Once again: An exercise in humility**

Having looked at the issues surrounding the topic of perfection, I hope some things have become clear. We have found that at times the biblical evidence points in different directions, and we discovered that this is also the case when we examine the many statements by Ellen White. I believe I have made a solid case for the position that the biblical concept of perfection is not to be equated with sinlessness. I also believe that I have sufficiently demonstrated how striving for perfection almost inevitably carries the insidious danger of legalism.

When all is said and done, we must admit that we will always be, at least to a certain degree, subjective in the way we approach the available material, and that we tend to emphasize in particular the things that we ourselves find very important and that confirm the ideas we had all along. And, therefore, I accept that, although I can honestly say that I have treated all the data as honestly as I can, this chapter is not the last word on the subject of biblical perfection.

---

[43]Marvin Moore, *How to Think About the End Time* (Nampa, ID: Pacific Press Pub. Assn., 2001), p. 188.

In the meantime, let us not only realize our limitations in our interpretation the Bible, but let us realize in particular our sinfulness. I must admit that sinless perfection is far away for me, and not just for me! Like Paul, I cannot claim that I have almost reached the state God wants me to be, and like him I must admit that I all too frequently do the very things I do not want to do! In all humility I must admit my own shortcoming and imperfections, looking towards Christ for my salvation. Experience has made sufficiently clear to me that things hopelessly derail if I trust in myself. In the end I know I cannot expect to reach a state of perfection this side of the second coming of Christ, but I must put all my trust in the perfect work Christ did on my behalf.

# APPENDIX

## Comments of Ellen G. White on Perfection

### Sinless Perfection?

God's ideal for His children is higher than the highest human thought can reach. "Be ye therefore perfect, even as your Father which is in heaven is perfect." This command is a promise. The plan of redemption contemplates our complete recovery from the power of Satan. Christ always separates the contrite soul from sin. He came to destroy the works of the devil, and He has made provision that the Holy Spirit shall be imparted to every repentant soul, to keep him from sinning.

The tempter's agency is not to be accounted an excuse for one wrong act. Satan is jubilant when he hears the professed followers of Christ making excuses for their deformity of character. It is these excuses that lead to sin. There is no excuse for sinning. A holy temper, a Christlike life, is accessible to every repenting, believing child of God.

The ideal of Christian character is Christlikeness. As the Son of man was perfect in His life, so His followers are to be perfect in their life. Jesus was in all things made like unto His brethren. He became flesh, even as we are. He was hungry and thirsty and weary. He was sustained by food and refreshed by sleep. He shared the lot of man; yet He was the blameless Son of God. He was God in the flesh. His character is to be ours. The Lord says of those who believe in Him, "I will dwell in them, and walk in them; and I will be their God, and they shall be My people." 2 Corinthians 6:16.

Christ is the ladder that Jacob saw, the base resting on the earth, and the topmost round reaching to the gate of heaven, to the very threshold of glory. If that ladder had failed by a single step of reaching the earth, we should have been lost. But Christ reaches us where we are. He took our nature and overcame, that we through taking His nature might overcome. Made "in the likeness of sinful flesh" (Romans 8:3), He lived a sinless life. Now by His divinity He lays hold

upon the throne of heaven, while by His humanity He reaches us. He bids us by faith in Him attain to the glory of the character of God. Therefore are we to be perfect, even as our "Father which is in heaven is perfect."
*The Desire of Ages*, pp. 311-312

It is the Spirit that makes effectual what has been wrought out by the world's Redeemer. It is by the Spirit that the heart is made pure. Through the Spirit the believer becomes a partaker of the divine nature. Christ has given His Spirit as a divine power to overcome all hereditary and cultivated tendencies to evil, and to impress His own character upon His church.

Of the Spirit Jesus said, "He shall glorify Me." The Savior came to glorify the Father by the demonstration of His love; so the Spirit was to glorify Christ by revealing His grace to the world. The very image of God is to be reproduced in humanity. The honor of God, the honor of Christ, is involved in the perfection of the character of His people.
*The Desire of Ages*, p. 671

Christ was the only sinless one who ever dwelt on earth; yet for nearly thirty years He lived among the wicked inhabitants of Nazareth. This fact is a rebuke to those who think themselves dependent upon place, fortune, or prosperity, in order to live a blameless life. Temptation, poverty, adversity, is the very discipline needed to develop purity and firmness.
*The Desire of Ages*, p. 72

Those who believe on Christ and obey His commandments are not under bondage to God's law; for to those who believe and obey, His law is not a law of bondage, but of liberty. Every one who believes on Christ, every one who relies on the keeping power of a risen Savior that has suffered the penalty pronounced upon the transgressor, every one who resists temptation and in the midst of evil copies the pattern given in the Christ-life, will through faith in the atoning sacrifice of Christ become a partaker of the divine nature, having escaped the corruption that is in the world through lust. Every one who by faith

obeys God's commandments, will reach the condition of sinlessness in which Adam lived before his transgression.
*The Signs of the Times*, July 23, 1902

It is sin that alienates from God. "Whosoever committeth sin transgresseth also the law: for sin is the transgression of the law. And ye know that he was manifested to take away our sins; and in him is no sin. Whosoever abideth in him sinneth not: whoso sinneth hath not seen him, neither known him."

To every one who surrenders fully to God is given the privilege of living without sin, in obedience to the law of heaven.
*The Review and Herald,* Sept. 27, 1906

In His teachings, Christ showed how far-reaching are the principles of the law spoken from Sinai. He made a living application of that law whose principles remain forever the great standard of righteousness—the standard by which all shall be judged in that great day when the judgment shall sit, and the books shall be opened. He came to fulfill all righteousness, and, as the head of humanity, to show man that he can do the same work, meeting every specification of the requirements of God. Through the measure of His grace furnished to the human agent, not one need miss heaven. Perfection of character is attainable by every one who strives for it. This is made the very foundation of the new covenant of the gospel. The law of Jehovah is the tree; the gospel is the fragrant blossoms and fruit which it bears.
*Selected Messages*, vol. 1, pp. 211-212

God will accept only those who are determined to aim high. He places every human agent under obligation to do his best. Moral perfection is required of all. Never should we lower the standard of righteousness in order to accommodate inherited or cultivated tendencies to wrong-doing. We need to understand that imperfection of character is sin. All righteous attributes of character dwell in God as a perfect, harmonious whole, and every one who receives Christ as a personal Savior is privileged to possess these attributes.
*Christ's Object Lessons*, p. 330

### Perfection as a Process and Direction of Life

The closer you come to Jesus, the more faulty you will appear in your own eyes; for your vision will be clearer, and your imperfections will be seen in broad and distinct contrast to His perfect nature. This is evidence that Satan's delusions have lost their power; that the vivifying influence of the Spirit of God is arousing you.

No deep-seated love for Jesus can dwell in the heart that does not realize its own sinfulness. The soul that is transformed by the grace of Christ will admire His divine character; but if we do not see our own moral deformity, it is unmistakable evidence that we have not had a view of the beauty and excellence of Christ.

The less we see to esteem in ourselves, the more we shall see to esteem in the infinite purity and loveliness of our Savior. A view of our sinfulness drives us to Him who can pardon; and when the soul, realizing its helplessness, reaches out after Christ, He will reveal Himself in power. The more our sense of need drives us to Him and to the word of God, the more exalted views we shall have of His character, and the more fully we shall reflect His image.
*Steps to Christ,* pp. 64-65

True sanctification unites believers to Christ and to one another in bonds of tender sympathy. This union causes to flow continually into the heart rich currents of Christlike love, which flows forth again in love for one another.

The qualities which it is essential for all to possess are those which marked the completeness of Christ's character,—His love, His patience, His unselfishness, and His goodness. These attributes are gained by doing kindly actions with a kindly heart.... Christians love those around them as precious souls for whom Christ has died. There is no such thing as a loveless Christian; for "God is love."
*Sons and Daughters of God,* p. 102

The specific place appointed us in life is determined by our capabilities. Not all reach the same development or do with equal efficiency the same work. God does not expect the hyssop to attain the propor-

tions of the cedar, or the olive the height of the stately palm. But each should aim just as high as the union of human with divine power makes it possible for him to reach.
*Education*, p. 267

Even the most perfect Christian may increase continually in the knowledge and love of God. 2 Peter 3:14, 18: "Wherefore, beloved, seeing that ye look for such things, be diligent that ye may be found of Him in peace, without spot, and blameless." "But grow in grace, and in the knowledge of our Lord and Savior Jesus Christ. To Him be glory both now and forever. Amen."

Sanctification is not the work of a moment, an hour, or a day. It is a continual growth in grace. We know not one day how strong will be our conflict the next. Satan lives, and is active, and every day we need to cry earnestly to God for help and strength to resist him. As long as Satan reigns we shall have self to subdue, besetments to overcome, and there is no stopping place, there is no point to which we can come and say we have fully attained.

Philippians 3:12: "Not as though I had already attained, either were already perfect: but I follow after, if that I may apprehend that for which also I am apprehended of Christ Jesus."

The Christian life is constantly an onward march. Jesus sits as a refiner and purifier of His people; and when His image is perfectly reflected in them, they are perfect and holy, and prepared for translation. A great work is required of the Christian. We are exhorted to cleanse ourselves from all filthiness of the flesh and spirit, perfecting holiness in the fear of God. Here we see where the great labor rests. There is a constant work for the Christian. Every branch in the parent vine must derive life and strength from that vine, in order to yield fruit.
*Testimonies for the Church*, vol. 1, p. 340

The germination of the seed represents the beginning of spiritual life, and the development of the plant is a beautiful figure of Christian growth. As in nature, so in grace; there can be no life without growth. The plant must either grow or die. As its growth is silent and imper-

ceptible, but continuous, so is the development of the Christian life. At every stage of development our life may be perfect; yet if God's purpose for us is fulfilled, there will be continual advancement. Sanctification is the work of a lifetime. As our opportunities multiply, our experience will enlarge.
    *Christ's Object Lessons*, p. 65

With our limited powers we are to be as holy in our sphere as God is holy in His sphere. To the extent of our ability, we are to make manifest the truth and love and excellence of the divine character. As wax takes the impression of the seal, so the soul is to take the impression of the Spirit of God and retain the image of Christ.

    We are to grow daily in spiritual loveliness. We shall fail often in our efforts to copy the divine pattern. We shall often have to bow down to weep at the feet of Jesus, because of our shortcomings and mistakes; but we are not to be discouraged; we are to pray more fervently, believe more fully, and try again with more steadfastness to grow into the likeness of our Lord. As we distrust our own power, we shall trust the power of our Redeemer, and render praise to God, who is the health of our countenance, and our God.

    Wherever there is union with Christ there is love. Whatever other fruits we may bear, if love be missing, they profit nothing. Love to God and our neighbor is the very essence of our religion. No one can love Christ and not love His children. When we are united to Christ, we have the mind of Christ. Purity and love shine forth in the character, meekness and truth control the life.
    *Selected Messages*, vol. 1, p. 337

There can be no growth or fruitfulness in the life that is centered in self. If you have accepted Christ as a personal Savior, you are to forget yourself, and try to help others. Talk of the love of Christ, tell of His goodness. Do every duty that presents itself. Carry the burden of souls upon your heart, and by every means in your power seek to save the lost. As you receive the Spirit of Christ—the Spirit of unselfish love and labor for others—you will grow and bring forth fruit. The graces of the Spirit will ripen in your character. Your faith will increase, your convictions deepen, your love be made perfect. More and more you will reflect the likeness of Christ in all that is pure, noble, and lovely.

"The fruit of the Spirit is love, joy, peace, longsuffering gentleness, goodness, faith, meekness, temperance." Gal. 5:22, 23. This fruit can never perish, but will produce after its kind a harvest unto eternal life.
*Christ's Object Lessons*, pp. 67-69

John declares, "If we say that we have not sinned, we make him a liar, and his word is not in us." But we are to accept the precious promise that, "if we confess our sins, he is faithful and just to forgive us our sins, and to cleanse us from all unrighteousness." We shall make manifest by our works as to whether or not we have personal faith in Christ as our Savior; for it is by the righteousness of Christ that we are sanctified. We are day by day to study the lessons of Christ, and grow up into him in all things. If we follow on to know the Lord, we shall know that his goings forth are prepared as the morning. He is perfecting Christian character after the divine model, is growing in faith, in influence and power, and this work will progress in his character until faith is lost in sight, and grace in glory. The righteousness of Christ is imputed to the obedient soul, and the peace of Christ is an abiding principle in the heart.
*The Signs of the Times*, May 16, 1895

Here is a special direction to deal tenderly with those overtaken in a fault. "Overtaken" must have its full significance.... To be led into sin unawares—not intending to sin, but to sin through want of watchfulness and prayer, not discerning the temptation of Satan and so falling into his snare—is very different from the one who plans and deliberately enters into temptation and plans out a course of sin.
*Our High Calling*, p. 177

Love is the basis of godliness. Whatever the profession, no man has pure love to God unless he has unselfish love for his brother. But we can never come into possession of this spirit by *trying* to love others. What is needed is the love of Christ in the heart. When self is merged

in Christ, love springs forth spontaneously. The completeness of Christian character is attained when the impulse to help and bless others springs constantly from within—when the sunshine of heaven fills the heart and is revealed in the countenance.
*Christ's Object Lessons*, p. 384

It is the Spirit that makes effectual what has been wrought out by the world's Redeemer. It is by the Spirit that the heart is made pure. Through the Spirit the believer becomes a partaker of the divine nature. Christ has given His Spirit as a divine power to overcome all hereditary and cultivated tendencies to evil, and to impress His own character upon His church.

Of the Spirit Jesus said, "He shall glorify Me." The Savior came to glorify the Father by the demonstration of His love; so the Spirit was to glorify Christ by revealing His grace to the world. The very image of God is to be reproduced in humanity. The honor of God, the honor of Christ, is involved in the perfection of the character of His people.
*The Desire of Ages*, p. 671

Let not God be dishonored by the proclamation from human lips, declaring, "I am sinless. I am holy." Sanctified lips will never give utterance to such presumptuous words.
*The Signs of the Times*, May 23, 1895

Christ is our pattern, the perfect and holy example that has been given us to follow. We can never equal the pattern; but we may imitate and resemble it according to our ability. When we fall, all helpless, suffering in consequence of our realization of the sinfulness of sin; when we humble ourselves before God, afflicting our souls by true repentance and contrition; when we offer our fervent prayers to God in the name of Christ, we shall as surely be received by the Father, as we sincerely make a complete surrender of our all to God. We should realize in our inmost soul that all our efforts in and of ourselves will be utterly worthless; for it is only in the name and strength of the Conqueror that we shall be overcomers.
*Review and Herald*, Feb. 5, 1895

# Chapter 7

# "Shaken" and on Our Own?

The topic of Last Generation Theology is, as we have seen, closely linked to the larger spectrum of last-day events. From the very beginning of their movement many Adventists have tried to make a catalogue of the main events that will happen at the end of time and to put them in their precise order. In his book *Preparing for the Final Crisis* Professor Fernando Chaij, a well-known Adventist author in the domain of apocalyptic prophecy, has listed the 10 most important final events: 1) a reform movement in the church; 2) the "sealing" of the believers; 3) the outpouring of the Holy Spirit power in the "latter rain"; 4) the last evangelistic boost in the "loud cry"; 5) the "shaking"; 6) the early time of trouble; 7) the close of probation; 8) the seven last plagues of Revelation 16; 9) the return of Christ; 10) the beginning of the 1000-year period of Revelation 20.[1]

Fernando Chaij does not insist that these events will occur exactly in this order. Other writers on this topic add additional events, such as a "death decree" for the true Sabbath-keeping remnant, and they profess to know exactly in what sequence the final events on earth will take place. Throughout Adventist history very detailed charts have been produced that show not only the exact order of these events but

---
[1] Fernando Chaij, *Preparing for the Final Crisis* (Nampa, ID: Pacific Press Pub. Assn., 1998), pp. 26-161.

also give detailed information about the overall time frame.

In 1842 Charles Fitch, a prominent leader in the Millerite movement, suggested that, following the example of Habakkuk, the prophetic visions should be written on "tables."[2] Perhaps the most famous of these tables was a chart that was produced as early as 1843. For many this chart remains the only solid basis for all reliable end-time projections. Ellen White clearly endorsed this graphic presentation of final events when she wrote: "I have seen that the 1843 chart was directed by the hand of the Lord, and that it should not be altered; that the figures [of the prophetic periods] were as He wanted them."[3] Other charts were subsequently produced (to which Ellen White did not object), and in some segments of the church the attempts to fit all end-time events, as Adventists have traditionally identified them, into one great visual chart are as popular today as they have been in the past.

These charts seem indeed to have a great appeal to a significant number of people. They say that these charts help them to really come to grips with the Adventist message for our present times. Others wonder whether this kind of timetable approach to the prophetic parts of the Bible is useful or even legitimate. Personally, I have two problems with this approach. First, I am not so sure that the biblical evidence is strong enough to provide us with all the details included in these timetables, with all the precise information about the time aspects, and with the exact order in which they are supposed to occur. In this chapter we will touch upon this issue. The second and perhaps even weightier problem that I have with this approach will have to wait until the next chapter. This second objection can be sum-

---

[2] EGW, *The Great Controversy* (1911 edition), p. 392.
[3] EGW, *Early Writings*, p. 74. See also Leroy E. Froom, "Historical Data on the '1843' Chart," *Ministry*, May 1942.

marized in a simple question: How can the second coming of Christ be "sudden" and "as a thief in the night," if a whole list of events must first take place?

**The shaking**

Among the events that are part of the Adventist end-time scenario that impact specifically on Last Generation Theology are the shaking and the close of probation. Let us first look at the shaking. This concept refers to the belief that immediately prior to the second coming many (or most?) Adventists will abandon their faith and their church because of "indifference, satanic deceptions, and the pressure of circumstances."[4] Ellen White has mentioned four causes for this shaking: 1) believers becoming disheartened because of persecution from forces outside of the church; 2) false theories from within the church; 3) a growing worldliness in the church; and 4) resistance to the prophetic writings, including her own.[5]

What is the basis for believing that such a shaking will take place? A few biblical statements are often quoted in connection with the concept of a future shaking. Some explicitly mention the term "shaking," but the exact terminology varies depending on the Bible version that is consulted. I will use italics for emphasis.

- Amos 9:9: "For I will give the command, and I will *shake* the people of Israel among all the nations as grain is shaken in a sieve, and not a pebble will reach the ground" (NIV). The KJV refers to a sifting rather than a shaking.
- Isaiah 17:5-6: "It will be as when reapers harvest the stand-

---

[4] "Shaking Time," in Don F. Neufeld, ed., *Seventh-day Adventist Encyclopedia* (Hagerstown, MD: Review and Herald Pub. Assn., 1996 edition), vol. 2, pp. 598-599.
[5] Roger W. Coon, "Shaking," in Denis Fortin and Jerry Moon, eds., *The Ellen G. White Encyclopedia*, pp. 1157-1158.

ing grain, gathering the grain in their arms—as when someone gleans heads of grain in the Valley of Rephaim. Yet some gleanings will remain, as when an olive tree is *beaten* [KJV: *shaken*], leaving two or three olives on the topmost branches, four or five on the fruitful boughs,' declares the LORD, the God of Israel" (NIV).

- Ezekiel 38:18-19: "And it shall come to pass at the same time when Gog shall come against the land of Israel, saith the Lord God, that my fury shall come up in my face. For in my jealousy and in the fire of my wrath I have spoken. Surely in that day there shall be a great *shaking* in the land of Israel" (KJV).

- Hebrews 12:26-29: "At that time his voice shook the earth, but now he has promised, 'Once more I will *shake* not only the earth but also the heavens.' The words 'once more' indicate the removing of what can be *shaken*—that is, created things—so that what cannot be *shaken* may remain. Therefore, since we are receiving a kingdom that cannot be *shaken*, let us be thankful, and so worship God acceptably with reverence and awe, for our 'God is a consuming fire'" (NIV).

- Revelation 6:12-13: "I watched as he opened the sixth seal. There was a great earthquake. The sun turned black like sackcloth made of goat hair, the whole moon turned blood red, and the stars in the sky fell to earth, as figs drop from a fig tree when *shaken* by a strong wind" (NIV).

- 2 Thessalonians 2:1-3: "Now we beseech you, brethren,... that ye be not soon *shaken* in mind, or be troubled, neither by spirit, nor by word, nor by letter as from us, as that the day of Christ is at hand. Let no man deceive you by any means: for that day shall not come, except there come a falling away first" (KJV).

I must admit that in reading these texts in which the term "shaking" occurs, I do not immediately make the connection with the traditional Adventist understanding of a shaking that will starkly reduce the body of believers at the end of time. The prophets addressed the Old Testament passages to the people of God in their times, and these texts cannot, in my view, be applied one-on-one to the time of the end, just before the second coming of Christ.

It is interesting to see how the *Seventh-day Adventist Bible Commentary* interprets these passages. There is no suggestion of an end-time application for the texts in Amos and Isaiah. The comment on the passage in Ezekiel does make an end-time application, but links it to the "fearful convulsions of nature that will precede the coming of the Son of man."[6] In its comments on the passage in Hebrews, the emphasis of the *Commentary* is on the physical shaking of the earth at the time of the giving of the Ten Commandments on Mount Sinai and the physical shaking of nature prior to the return of Christ. "This present world and all that is in it will pass away."[7] It is also quite clear that the shaking referred to in Revelation 6 must also be understood in that sense.

2 Thessalonians 2:2-3 refers to people at the end of time who are in danger of being shaken and does indeed foretell that there will be a "falling away" of many. But it does not inform us how and when this process will take place.

It would seem that (to state it kindly) there is only very limited direct biblical support for the concept of an end-time shaking, and certainly not for the idea that such a shaking is the tool that God will use to reduce the Adventist Church to a faithful remnant that is, or can become, the select "last generation" of believers who "perfectly

---

[6]*The Seventh-day Adventist Bible Commentary*, vol. 4, p. 709.
[7]*Ibid.*, vol. 7, p. 488.

reflect" the character of Christ.

As I studied this topic quite carefully, I was not only amazed to see the slim biblical evidence but also to discover that most of the mainline Adventist authors on end-time events have very little to say about this kind of a shaking. Take, for instance, the 500-plus-page book by Norman Gulley, one of the most respected theologians of the Adventist Church in the last few decades. In his book *Christ is Coming: A Christ-Centered Approach to Last-Day Events*[8] he provides us with an in-depth study of final events. (I believe there is a rather general consensus that he is on the more conservative rather than on the more liberal side of the Adventist theological spectrum.) I could not find any mention of the shaking in this book. And neither does it appear in the widely respected *Handbook of Seventh-day Adventist Theology*.[9]

The only well known mainline Adventist theologian who has focused on the "shaking" theme is—as far as I know—Marvin Moore, a longtime editor of the Adventist journal *The Signs of the Times* and a prolific writer on Bible prophecy. In a 10-page chapter in one of his books about the end of time, entitled "The Shaking,"[10] Moore mentions only two biblical passages, both from Matthew 24 (verses 24-25 and 37-39), which can only in a very indirect way be connected to a "shaking." Most of the 10 pages are filled with quotations from Ellen White, on which Moore's argument about the shaking is built. He defines the shaking as the "time when those who are not genuine Christians will be shaken out of the church."

Most publications in which the idea of an end-time shaking fig-

---

[8] Published by the Review and Herald Pub. Assn. (Hagerstown, MD, 1998).
[9] Written by a group of prominent Adventist theologians and edited by Raoul Dederen. Published as the 12th volume of the Commentary Reference Series (Hagerstown: Review and Herald Pub. Assn., 2000).
[10] Marvin Moore, *The Crisis of the End Time* (Boise, ID: Pacific Press Pub. Assn., 1992), pp. 181-190.

ures more prominently are found at the conservative fringe of the church, from authors such as Kevin Hayden, Dennis Priebe, and Larry Kilpatrick.

**Ellen G. White and the shaking**

If there is such a slim biblical basis for the expectation of a shaking at the very end of time, we may well ask how it is to be explained that many Adventist preachers and writers have so much to say about it. The answer is that they find this information in the Ellen G. White writings. It is reported that in a vision in 1857 Ellen White "was shown the people of God, and saw them mightily shaken." The description of this vision is found in a number of her early publications. I will quote from the first volume of the *Testimonies to the Church*, where she describes what she saw in graphic terms:

> Some, with strong faith and agonizing cries, were pleading with God. Their countenances were pale, and marked with deep anxiety, expressive of their internal struggle. Firmness and great earnestness were expressed in their countenances, while large drops of perspiration fell from their foreheads. Now and then their faces would light up with the marks of God's approbation, and again the same solemn, earnest, anxious look would settle upon them. [With references to Joel 2:15-17; James 4:7-10; Zephaniah 2:1-3.]
>
> Evil angels crowded around them, pressing their darkness upon them, to shut out Jesus from their view, that their eyes might be drawn to the darkness that surrounded them, and they distrust God and next murmur against Him. Their only safety was in keeping their eyes directed upward. An-

gels of God had charge over His people, and as the poisonous atmosphere from the evil angels was pressed around these anxious ones, the heavenly angels were continually wafting their wings over them, to scatter the thick darkness. Some, I saw, did not participate in this work of agonizing and pleading. They seemed indifferent and careless. They were not resisting the darkness around them, and it shut them in like a thick cloud....

I asked the meaning of the shaking I had seen, and was shown that it would be caused by the straight testimony called forth by the counsel of the True Witness to the Laodiceans....

The testimony of the True Witness has not been half heeded. The solemn testimony upon which the destiny of the church hangs has been lightly esteemed, if not entirely disregarded....

The careless and indifferent, who did not join with those who prized victory and salvation enough to perseveringly plead and agonize for it, did not obtain it, and they were left behind in darkness.[11]

In her book *The Great Controversy* we find a statement that is often quoted in connection with the shaking:

As the storm approaches, a large class who have professed faith in the third angel's message, but have not been sanctified through obedience to the truth, abandon their position and join the ranks of the opposition.[12]

---
[11] EGW, *Testimonies for the Church*, vol. 1, pp. 179-181.
[12] EGW, *The Great Controversy*, p. 608.

A good overview of what Ellen G. White has written about the shaking is found in a relatively recent compilation of her statements on final events. It has a chapter about this subject, entitled *The Shaking*, with the subtitle: "Church Membership no Guarantee of Salvation."[13] As is the case with all compilations of Ellen White materials, the context is largely lacking, but this chapter, nonetheless, gives a good idea of what she said on this topic, although the term "shaking" is not always used. I will quote a few samples—many other quotes have a similar message.

> It is a solemn statement that I make to the church, that not one in twenty whose names are registered upon the church books are prepared to close their earthly history, and would be as verily without God and without hope in the world as the common sinner.[14]

> There will be a shaking of the sieve. The chaff must in time be separated from the wheat. Because iniquity abounds, the love of many waxes cold. It is the very time when the genuine will be the strongest.[15]

> The history of the rebellion of Dathan and Abiram is being repeated, and will be repeated till the close of time. Who will be on the Lord's side? Who will be deceived, and in their turn become deceivers?[16]

---

[13] EGW, *Last Day Events*, pp. 172-182.
[14] EGW, *Christian Service*, p. 41.
[15] EGW, Letter 46 (April 22, 1887).
[16] EGW, Letter 15 (June 27, 1892).

> As trials thicken around us, both separation and unity will be seen in our ranks. Some who are now ready to take up weapons of warfare will in times of real peril make it manifest that they have not built upon the solid rock; they will yield to temptation. Those who have had great light and precious privileges, but have not improved them, will, under one pretext or another, go out from us.[17]

It is interesting to note what Ellen White says about the *time* of the shaking. In most of her statements she, directly or indirectly, simply refers to the (still future) end of time. But note the statements below. In 1882 she said that the time for this shaking or sifting of the church is "not far distant." In 1895 she expresses the same thought, but five years later she warns that "we are in the shaking time."

> The time is not far distant when the test will come to every soul. The mark of the beast will be urged upon us. Those who have step by step yielded to worldly demands and conformed to worldly customs will not find it a hard matter to yield to the powers that be, rather than subject themselves to derision, insult, threatened imprisonment, and death. The contest is between the commandments of God and the commandments of men. In this time the gold will be separated from the dross in the church.[18]

> The Lord is soon to come; there must be a refining, winnowing process in every church, for there are among us wicked

---

[17] EGW, *Testimonies for the Church*, vol. 6, p. 400.
[18] EGW, *Testimonies for the Church*, vol. 5, p. 81.

men who do not love the truth.[19]

We are in the shaking time, the time when everything that can be shaken will be shaken. The Lord will not excuse those who know the truth if they do not in word and deed obey His commands.[20]

So, what do we conclude from this discussion of the shaking, on the basis of the biblical evidence and the comments from the pen of Ellen White? In the final paragraphs of this chapter I will return to that question.

### The close of probation

A possibly even more important concept in connection with Last Generation Theology is that of the close of probation. Other Christians may wonder what Adventists mean by that expression, but for Seventh-day Adventists themselves this is a term they constantly use. Linguistic philosophers would say that the term is part of the Adventist "language game." But what does the term mean?

The *SDA Encyclopedia* defines "probation" as "the opportunity provided humanity in which to accept divine grace and to prepare for eternal life, and the time allotted for this purpose."[21] In other words, it is the possibility to come to Christ and be saved. Our individual probation closes when we die. There is no biblical basis whatsoever for the idea that we might still get another chance after death. When we die our eternal fate is sealed. But, so Adventists argue, just before the second coming of Christ the term "probation" acquires a special

---

[19] EGW, *The Review and Herald*, March 19, 1895.
[20] EGW, *Testimonies for the Church*, vol. 6, p. 331.
[21] "Probation," in *Seventh-day Adventist Encyclopedia*, vol. 2, p. 383.

connotation. Probation will "close" when all people have clearly made the choice for or against Christ. This is what the decree of Revelation 22:11 is all about: "Let the one who does wrong continue to do wrong; let the vile person continue to be vile; let the one who does right continue to do right; and let the holy person continue to be holy." The line between God's people and those who have turned against Him is drawn, and this marks "the close of probation."

That probation will close a short time before Christ's return is obvious, so Adventists believe, from a careful study of Revelation 14, 15, and 16.[22] Revelation 16 describes the seven last plagues, which will, as the context shows, be "poured out" just prior to the second coming. In chapter 15 we read about God's temple in heaven, which opens as the seven angels, who are to pour out the plagues, appear. At that moment the temple fills with smoke from the glory of God, and the temple is no longer accessible until the plagues have been poured out (Revelation 15:8). Further light on what this means may be gleaned, we are told, from the Old Testament sanctuary service. At the time of the dedication of the temple of Solomon, this building was filled with a cloud, and as a result the priests could no longer perform their ministry (2 Chronicles 5:13-14; also 2 Chronicles 7:1-2). This foreshadowed the phase in Christ's ministry in the heavenly temple, when the heavenly High Priest can no longer remain in the heavenly most holy place and must cease His intercessory work as our Mediator.

Seventh-day Adventists have developed the doctrine of the heavenly sanctuary. It states that after His ascension Jesus began to min-

---

[22] See the chapter "The Close of Probation" in Marvin Moore, *How to Think About the End Time*, pp. 143-153. Others are not convinced that the Revelation is explicit about the time of the close of probation. See, e.g., Jon Paulien, *What the Bible Says About the End-Time* (Hagerstown, MD: Review and Herald Pub. Assn., 1994), p. 148.

ister in the heavenly sanctuary. But from 1844 onwards, they believe, He has been engaged in a special work in the second apartment of this sanctuary. It is the heavenly Day of Atonement that was foreshadowed by the yearly Day of Atonement ceremonies in the Old Testament tabernacle and, subsequently, in the Jerusalem temple. The prophecies of Daniel 8 and 9 deal with the cleansing of a sanctuary, and this is applied to the heavenly sanctuary. Moreover, the judgment aspect of the earthly Day of Atonement prefigured the high-priestly work of Christ in a pre-Advent judgment, in which the merits of Jesus' death on the cross are applied to those who will inherit eternal life. There are plenty of publications in the Adventist Church that explain this, admittedly, rather complicated doctrine.[23]

The close of probation has a very serious implication. There comes, according to the Adventist understanding of final events, a moment when all people have either received the "mark of the beast" or God's "seal" of approval. The heavenly High Priest finishes His work. There is no longer a Mediator. The seven last plagues will fall on the earth and torture the global population. And, according to Last Generation Theology, this is the time when there will be a final perfect generation—the ultimate remnant.

Here again most of our information must be derived from Ellen White, and once again the compilation *Last Day Events* makes many of the important statements easily accessible.[24] Here is a small sample:

---

[23]See, e.g., M.L. Andreasen, *The Sanctuary Service* (Washington, DC: Review and Herald Pub. Assn., 1937); Roy Adams, *The Sanctuary: Understanding the Heart of Adventist Theology* (Hagerstown, MD: Review and Herald Pub. Assn., 1993); Marvin Moore, *The Case for the Investigative Judgment: Its Biblical Foundation* (Nampa, ID: Pacific Press Pub. Assn., 2010); Arnold V. Wallenkampf and W. Richard Lesher, *The Sanctuary and the Atonement: Biblical, Historical and Theological Studies* (General Conf. of SDA, Biblical Research Institute, 1981); Clifford Goldstein, *1844 Made Simple* (Nampa, ID: Pacific Press Pub. Assn., 1998); Angel Manuel Rodriguez, "The Sanctuary," in Raoul Dederen, ed., *Handbook of Seventh-day Adventist Theology*, pp. 375-417.
[24]EGW, *Last Day Events*, pp. 227-237.

God has not revealed to us the time when this message will close, or when probation will have an end. Those things that are revealed we shall accept for ourselves and for our children; but let us not seek to know that which has been kept secret in the councils of the Almighty....

Letters have come to me asking me if I have any special light as to the time when probation will close; and I answer that I have only this message to bear, that it is now time to work while the day lasts, for the night cometh in which no man can work.[25]

An angel returning from the earth announces that his work is done; the final test has been brought upon the world, and all who have proved themselves loyal to the divine precepts have received "the seal of the living God." Then Jesus ceases His intercession in the sanctuary above. He lifts His hands, and with a loud voice says, "It is done."[26]

When the work of the investigative judgment closes, the destiny of all will have been decided for life or death. Probation is ended a short time before the appearing of the Lord in the clouds of heaven....

Before the Flood, after Noah entered the ark, God shut him in and shut the ungodly out; but for seven days the people, knowing not that their doom was fixed, continued their careless, pleasure-loving life and mocked the warnings of impending judgment. "So," says the Saviour,

---

[25] EGW, *Selected Messages*, vol. 1, p. 191.
[26] EGW, *The Great Controversy*, p. 613.

"shall also the coming of the Son of man be" (Matthew 24:39). Silently, unnoticed as the midnight thief, will come the decisive hour which marks the fixing of every man's destiny, the final withdrawal of mercy's offer to guilty men....

While the man of business is absorbed in the pursuit of gain, while the pleasure lover is seeking indulgence, while the daughter of fashion is arranging her adornments—it may be in that hour the Judge of all the earth will pronounce the sentence: "Thou art weighed in the balances, and art found wanting."[27]

The ministers of God will have done their last work, offered their last prayers, shed their last bitter tear for a rebellious church and an ungodly people. Their last solemn warning has been given.

Oh, then how quickly would houses and lands, dollars that have been miserly hoarded and cherished and tightly grasped, be given for some consolation by those who have professed the truth and have not lived it out, for the way of salvation to be explained, or to hear a hopeful word, or a prayer, or an exhortation from their ministers. But no, they must hunger and thirst on in vain; their thirst will never be quenched, no consolation can they get; their cases are decided and eternally fixed. It is a fearful, awful time.[28]

In the time when God's judgments are falling without

---
[27]EGW, *The Great Controversy*, pp. 490-491.
[28]EGW, Manuscript 1, 1857.

> mercy, oh, how enviable to the wicked will be the position of those who abide "in the secret place of the Most High"—the pavilion in which the Lord hides all who have loved Him and have obeyed His commandments! The lot of the righteous is indeed an enviable one at such a time to those who are suffering because of their sins. But the door of mercy is closed to the wicked, no more prayers are offered in their behalf after probation ends. [29]

This last statement is quite remarkable. When probation has ended, Ellen White says, the wicked will have no place to go. They are eternally lost. They knock in vain on the "door of mercy." This is in stark contrast to those "who abide in the secret place of the Most High"—where the Lord hides all who have remained loyal to Him.

This should be an encouragement to all Seventh-day Adventists—whether or not they give credence to Last Generation Theology. Whatever happens and whatever this "close of probation" may imply, according to Ellen White there is no reason for anxiety. Those who will be saved will be protected! But how do we reconcile this with her statement in *The Great Controversy* that, when Jesus leaves the heavenly sanctuary, "*the righteous must live in the sight of a holy God without an intercessor*"?[30]

**Must we live without a Mediator?**

Many Adventists worry greatly about the close of probation. They have heard sermons and read books about its implications. It is commonly believed that there comes a moment when Christ no longer intercedes for us. We must live without a Mediator. In other words,

---
[29] EGW, in *The Seventh-day Adventist Bible Commentary*, vol. 3, p. 1150.
[30] EGW, *The Great Controversy*, p. 614.

we are on our own. Believers in Last Generation Theology hold that the final generation will by then have reached the state of perfection. Their sins are forgiven and, being perfect, it would seem that they no longer need Christ's intercession on their behalf. But what about those who do not agree with Last Generation Theology and believe that they will remain sinners until the very end of time and therefore will continue to need Christ's intercession on their behalf until the very end?

Do they indeed have reason for anxiety and despair? Marvin Moore argues that we are not left on our own.[31] We may find solace in the promise of Christ that the Holy Spirit will be with us forever (John 14:16-18). That gives courage, for we will need more of the power of the Spirit during that final cataclysmic period than ever before. Also, Christ did not promise His disciples, "I will be with you until the end of probation," but "I am with you always, to the very end of the age" (Matthew 28:20). Moore continues to assure us that it is in God's nature to forgive and that "if God's people need forgiveness in any sense after the close of probation, it will surely be available."[32] He adds, "The idea that our own righteousness will be sufficient following the close of probation is totally contrary to the gospel."[33] I find Moore's arguments quite compelling. Angel Manuel Rodriguez remains somewhat vague in answering the question of whether the believer will temporarily have to live without a Mediator, but he also seems to suggest that Christ's mediatorial work, or at least some aspects of it, will continue until Christ returns. This is what he says in an authoritative work on Adventist doctrine:

---

[31] Marvin Moore, *How to Think About the End Time*, pp. 146-149.
[32] *Ibid.*, p. 148.
[33] *Ibid.*

Every aspect of the Christian experience is mediated by Christ, who lives to intercede on behalf of those who approach God through Him. This aspect of the ministry of Christ will continue until He leaves the heavenly sanctuary at the Second Coming.[34]

**The latter rain, the loud cry, the remnant, and...**

The shaking and the close of probation are not the only parts of the Adventist end-time scenario that are important when dealing with Last Generation Theology. We could, for instance, also mention the so-called "latter rain." This term refers to the belief that prior to the return of Christ there will be an unparalleled outpouring of Holy Spirit power, with the accompanying result of large numbers of conversions, such as happened on the day of Pentecost, but on a much bigger scale (both events are seen as fulfillments of the prophecy in Joel 2:28-32). This, of course, happens before the close of probation. It is the last global evangelistic thrust. In Adventist thinking, this refers to the loud cry of the third angel in Revelation 14:9-12. It would seem that, while many are being supposedly shaken out of the church, a great number of people around the world make the right choice and, while "probation lingers," join the church.

Other terms one meets as one studies the Adventist understanding of the sequence of final events are "little time of trouble," "big time of trouble," "time of Jacob's trouble," "seal of God," "mark of the beast," "Sunday law," and "death decree." All these elements are linked to a short period, prior to the last plagues and the return of Christ.

A term with particular significance is that of the "remnant." For Last Generation Theology supporters it is clear that the final generation of

---

[34] Angel Manuel Rodriquez, "The Sanctuary," in *Handbook of Seventh-day Adventist Theology*, p. 393.

those who "perfectly reflect the character of Christ" are the ultimate embodiment of God's remnant people. Many others are not so sure how this remnant (i.e., the "rest" of the offspring of the woman, referred to in Revelation 12:17) is to be identified, and whether it is ever possible for us to know who exactly belongs to this remnant. Angel Rodriquez, a respected Adventist theologian and former director of the Biblical Research Institute in the headquarters office of the Adventist Church, reminds us that there are a number of different views in contemporary Adventism as to who constitutes the remnant.[35] At first Adventists usually saw themselves as this latter-day "rest" or remnant. A literal reading of the book of Revelation convinced many that the number was limited to the 144,000 of Revelation 7:1-8. Gradually (as the number of Adventists in the world increased sharply) the view prevailed that the number 144,000 has a symbolic significance and that the remnant could actually be much larger than this literal number. Others have warned against too much unfounded optimism; they tend to quote the statement by Ellen White in which she says that "not one in twenty whose names are registered upon the church books" will survive the shaking.[36] Yet other Adventist voices do not want to claim this remnant status exclusively for Adventists. Some Ellen White statements may actually be quoted in support of this view. Although the word "remnant" is not used, the following quote clearly points in that direction. At the end of a chapter in her book *Prophets and Kings* about Elijah's experiences, she makes an end-time application:

> Among earth's inhabitants, scattered in every land, there are those who have not bowed the knee to Baal. Like the stars

---
[35] See Angel Manuel Rodriguez, "The Remnant and the Adventist Church," www.adventistbiblicalresearch.org/sites/default/files/pdf/remnantSDAchurch_0.pdf.
[36] The statement was made in 1893. See EGW, *Christian Service*, p. 41.

of heaven, which appear only at night, these faithful ones will shine forth when darkness covers the earth and gross darkness the people. In heathen Africa, in the Catholic lands of Europe and of South America, in China, in India, in the islands of the sea, and in all the dark corners of the earth, God has in reserve a firmament of chosen ones that will yet shine forth amidst the darkness, revealing clearly to an apostate world the transforming power of obedience to His law.[37]

It would seem best not to lay too much stress on "who" constitute the remnant and not to move beyond the limited biblical data in defining the *identity* of the remnant. The essential thing is to be clear about the *characteristics* of the remnant.

Perhaps it would be best to focus on the clear characteristics that God's end-time people must exhibit: Obeying God and being firmly rooted in the faith of Christ—committed to the last-day mission to call the people all around the world to loyalty to their Creator. The most important question, today, for me as an individual, is: Are these characteristics evident in my life, and am I totally serious about communicating a saving faith to others?[38]

**Back to humility**

Our treatment of last-day events in the context of our discussion of Last Generation Theology cannot be exhaustive and cannot possibly deal with all these events in all their aspects. My tentative conclu-

---

[37] EGW, *Prophets and Kings,* pp. 188-189.
[38] Reinder Bruinsma, *The Body of Christ: A Biblical Understanding of the Church* (Hagerstown, MD: Review and Herald Pub. Assn., 2009), p. 201.

sion is this: We know that we are living at the end of time. We know that we must take our faith utterly seriously and build and maintain an ever-closer relationship with God. We also know that the world will be facing some very rough times and living as believers will be ever more challenging. But we also know that God is not yet done with this world and that He wants many more to accept salvation in Jesus Christ, with all this entails. In addition, we have ample biblical evidence for the undeniable fact that there comes a moment in the life of every individual when he/she must decide for or against Christ, and that at some point in time this possibility will no longer be there, and that, when Christ returns, only those who have committed their life to Him will be saved.

As to many of the aspects that we touched upon in this chapter, I strongly believe we must be reluctant to fill in all the details. As we saw, in many cases the biblical material is rather scanty; it is important that we do not read the Bible through Adventist spectacles only and make the biblical passages conform to what we want them to say, in conformity with our own cherished theories. We should not read the Bible to find confirmation for the views we already have, but come at the texts afresh and allow the Word to say what it has to say—nothing less but also nothing more (Revelation 22:18-19).

To what extent we use Ellen White as an authoritative source to fill in the gaps in our knowledge of end-time events depends on our view of her inspiration. The fact that she is not always consistent in what she said during her long ministry should be factored in into any appraisal. And could it be that some Adventist students of end-time events are guilty of treating Ellen White's statements as the "greater light," while she herself was adamant that she was only to be used as a "lesser light" that points us to the "greater light"?[39] The Bible must always remain the basis for all matters of doctrine.

There is a specific danger with regard to the way in which some Adventist circles view the shaking. It can easily lead to the idea that the tragic exodus from the church that we currently see, particularly in Western countries, is something unavoidable. And that it is, in fact, something positive: the earlier this shaking takes place, the sooner Christ returns. This line of thinking will preempt a critical analysis of why so many young people (as well as others of all age groups) leave the church.[40]

I repeat what I said in earlier chapters: Let us be careful not to pretend that we know everything that is yet to happen in every detail. Let us in all humility accept the fact that we know what has been clearly revealed to us but need to stay away from speculation about things that have not been fully revealed. I am afraid that many supporters of Last Generation Theology must develop more of that much needed humility.

---

[39] EGW, *The Review and Herald*, Jan. 20, 1903; EGW, *Selected Messages*, vol. 3, p. 30.
[40] See my recent book *Facing Doubt: A Book for Adventist Believers 'on the Margins,'* especially pp. 35-62.

# Chapter 8

# Can we "Hasten" the Second Coming?

The second coming of Christ is an extremely important theme in Last Generation Theology. As we saw, a key belief of Last Generation Theology is the conviction that Jesus Christ will not return to take His people home until there is a "final generation" that "perfectly reflects the character of Christ." In other words, the second coming will be delayed until this perfect remnant is in place! By implication this also means that the sooner this perfect last generation is constituted, the sooner Christ will come and the sooner our salvation will at last be fully realized. Therefore, it follows that it is crucial for God's people to do everything they can to "hasten" the coming of the Lord. That we can do this, according to Last Generation Theology supporters, is clear from 2 Peter 3:12, where we are admonished to look forward to the day of the Lord, and "speed its coming."

### We have this hope

Through the centuries Christians have looked for the return of Christ. At times the fervor was at a low ebb, but at other moments the thought that the second coming was near set the believers on fire. The immediate roots of the Adventist Church are found in the Millerite movement of the mid-19th century. The prediction of the Millerites that Christ would come in 1844 failed and led to the "great disappointment." The Millerite movement totally imploded, but a small group emerged that would continue to proclaim the nearness of the return of Christ, while rediscovering a number of other important biblical teachings. This group developed into the worldwide Seventh-day Adventist Church, which ever since has emphasized the Advent hope as one of the most important *raisons d'être*. "Christ is coming soon" remained a cardinal aspect of their gospel proclamation.

The Adventist pioneers firmly believed that the second coming was a matter of years, not decades or centuries. We can taste this sense of immediacy in some of the early statements of Ellen G. White. Referring to those who in 1856 were attending a gathering of Adventist believers, she quoted an angel who had informed her: "Some [will be] food for worms, some subjects of the seven last plagues, some will be alive and remain upon the earth to be translated at the coming of Jesus."[1] Somewhat later (in 1872) she stressed that "time is short" and that therefore "we should work with diligence and double energy. Our children may never enter college."[2] Four years later she made a similar statement: "It is really not wise to have children now. Time is short, the perils of the last days are upon us, and the little children will be largely swept off before this."[3] This sentiment was repeated in 1885: "In this age of the world, as the scenes of earth's history are soon to close and we are about to enter upon the time of trouble such as never was, the fewer

---

[1] EGW, *Testimonies for the Church*, vol. 1, pp. 131-132.
[2] EGW, *Testimonies for the Church*, vol. 3, p. 159.
[3] EGW, Letter 48 (1876).

the marriages contracted, the better for all, both men and women."[4]

Being a lifelong Adventist, who has now lived for more than seven decades, I can remember the very frequent sermons I heard in my childhood years that stressed the signs of the times. These were clear proof that we were now very near the end. When I went to college and began my studies to become a pastor, some of my fellow students were not so sure it was a good idea to spend four or five years in college. Would it not be much better to go out and tell the people about the soon coming of the Lord? In those days many Adventists believed they stood a good chance of being alive at that grand moment.

This sense of the immediacy of Jesus' return was shared by most Adventists of earlier generations. It has, however, been increasingly difficult to maintain this keen sense of expectancy of earlier generations of Adventists. Instead there is a widespread feeling of frustration or even doubt. Why does it take so long? Why this delay?

**Nearness and distance**

Before addressing the question of this delay of Christ's coming, it may be useful to say something about the apparent paradox we find in the Bible with regard to the time of the second coming.[5] Some texts emphasize the soonness of His coming, while other passages seem to indicate that it may take a while before Christ comes back.

We find this apparent paradox between "soon" and "not so soon" already in the Old Testament, where the "day of the Lord" and everything related to it is often described as something to be expected in the very near future. The end comes *this* week rather than *next* week,

---
[4] EGW, *Testimonies for the Church*, vol. 5, p. 366.
[5] Some sections in the remainder of the chapter are based on my book on the second coming that I wrote in the Dutch language: *Van Komst naar Wederkomst* (Huis ter Heide/Brussel: Uitgeverij Veritas, 1997), pp. 29-42.

today rather than tomorrow! But at the same time, however strange this may seem to our rationalistic western minds—with our emphasis on strict chronological order—these very same events are often pushed into a more distant, or even very far away, future. We find this tension, for instance, in the book of the prophet Amos. In Amos 1:3, 2:6, and 3:9-11 "the day of the Lord" is situated in the immediate future and linked to the judgment that may come any moment over Israel's neighbors. But in other passages (for instance Amos 7:4; 8:8-9; 9:13,15) the "day of the Lord" is placed in a rather more distant future.

We meet something similar with the prophet Zephaniah. He says in 1:14, "The great day of the Lord is near—near and coming quickly" (see also 2:1; 3:7). He is, however, much less specific about "the day I will stand up" in 3:8, 10. Isaiah tells his listeners to "wail, for the day of the Lord is near; it will come like destruction from the Almighty" (13:6). Yet in texts immediately preceding this statement "the day of the Lord" is placed in a much wider context, without creating the impression that it could take place any moment. These two different approaches to "the day of the Lord" in the Old Testament must be kept in mind as we try to find further information in the New Testament about the time aspect of Jesus' second coming.

A number of statements by Christ in the Gospels seem to convey the distinct impression that Jesus' disciples were to expect His second coming even during their lifetime. In Mark 9:1 (cf. Matthew 16:28; Luke 9:27) we read this remarkable statement that Jesus addressed to His disciples, "Truly I tell you, some who are standing here will not taste death before they see that the kingdom of God has come with power." We find similar words in Christ's famous discourse about the final events, "Truly I tell you, this generation will certainly not pass away until all these things have happened" (Mark 13:30; cf.

Matthew 24:34; Luke 21:32). And when Jesus sent His disciples on their mission of proclaiming the coming of the kingdom of God, He warned them about the difficulties they would have to face. But, He said, "When you are persecuted in one place, flee to another. Truly I tell you, you will not finish going through the towns of Israel before the Son of Man comes" (Matthew 10:23).

In the letters of Paul we also find several statements about the second coming of Jesus and the events related to it, which situate this event in the immediate future. In 1 Thessalonians 4:15-17 Paul counts himself among those who will experience the second coming. "We who are still alive and are left will be caught up together with them in the clouds to meet the Lord in the air. And so we will be with the Lord forever."

In his first letter to the Corinthians we find the same type of "we" texts: "We will not all sleep, but we will all be changed" (1 Corinthians 15:51-52). In this the same Paul urgently advises his single readers, just as Ellen G. White would do many centuries later, not to get married. "This world in its present form is passing away," he argues (1 Corinthians 7:31). The Philippians likewise had to realize that the coming of Christ was "near" (Philippians 4:5) and had to make sure to be "pure and blameless for the day of Christ" (1:10). In his letter to the Romans Paul insisted that "our salvation is nearer now than when we first believed" (Romans 13:11). And at the end of this letter he added, "The God of peace will soon crush Satan under your feet" (16:20).

Elsewhere in the New Testament we repeatedly find the same emphasis on the fact that salvation will be fully and finally realized in the immediate future. The writer of the book of Hebrews admonishes his readers not to give up "meeting together…and all the more as you see the Day approaching" (Hebrews 10:25). James had no doubt that the coming of the Lord was "near" (James 5:8-9), while, according to Peter, the temptations and sufferings of this present world would soon, after "a little while," be over (1 Peter 1:6; 5:10), since "the end of all things is near" (4:7). The Revelation of John time and time again underlines the same point (e.g., Revelation 1:1, 3; 3:11; 22:7, 12, 20).

The message that the end of the world and the second coming of Christ are "near" is an ever-recurring theme that runs like a golden thread through the New Testament. But other texts throw a slightly different light on this matter. Those statements of Christ, which create the impression that He Himself was of the opinion that His second coming would be no more than a few years in the future, must be read against the background of numerous other statements, which seem to allow for considerably more time between His first and His second coming.

The signs listed in Matthew 24 (cf. Mark 13; Luke 21) suggest that a number of historical processes would precede the end of the world. And even when some of the signs become visible, we are told, this does not mean the immediate end of all things (Matthew 24:6; Mark 13:7). In this connection we should also mention some of the parables. In the parable of the slave, appointed by his master to care for his belongings during his absence, we find the presupposition that the return of the Lord will require a considerable waiting time (Matthew 24:48; cf. Luke 12:41-48). In the parable of the wise and the foolish virgins, the bridegroom comes so late that all fall asleep (Matthew 25:5). The Lord, who in the parable of the talents entrusts his possession to his slaves before he goes abroad, only returns "after a long time" (Matthew 25:19).

When the rumor spread among Jesus' disciples that the kingdom of God was to appear at any moment, Jesus told the parable of "a man of noble birth" who "went to a distant country to have himself appointed king and then to return" (Luke 19:12). Three other parables about the kingdom of heaven suggest a process of some duration: the tares growing together with the wheat until harvest time; the mustard seed that slowly develops into a large tree; and the leaven that takes its time to penetrate all the dough (Matthew 13:24-33).

Some theologians argue that the three texts quoted earlier, in which Jesus places His return in the immediate future (Mark 9:1; 13:30; Matthew 10:23), simply indicate that Jesus was mistaken: His words were disproved by the passing of time. They suggest that the biblical passages that seem to allow for a longer period are later revisions by the Gospel writers. Many other theologians are, however, convinced there must be some other solution for the apparent contradiction. Mark 9:1 could refer to the transfiguration. Both Mark 9:1 and the parallel passages in Matthew and Luke seem to indicate that indeed the Gospel writers saw a connection between Jesus' statements about those who would see the kingdom before they would die and Jesus' transfiguration six days later. The phrase "this generation" in Mark 13:30, many biblical exegetes argue, does not necessarily apply to Jesus' actual hearers at that time but can be well explained in a somewhat broader context. The same is true for the "you" of Matthew 10:23.

In Paul's letters we not only find assurances that Jesus' coming is very near, there are also statements that seem to indicate that a somewhat longer period must first elapse. Addressing a group of elders who had come from Ephesus to Miletus, Paul discusses what would happen after his departure: "Savage wolves will come in among you and will not spare the flock" (Acts 20:29; cf. Peter's words in 2 Peter 3:3-5). In his second letter to the Thessalonians the apostle Paul refers to a particular problem in their church. Some believers in Thessaloniki had become "unsettled" and "alarmed," thinking that "the day of the Lord" had already come. Paul is anxious to correct that misunderstanding. Things will not go that quickly, he says, "for that day will not come until the rebellion occurs and the man of lawlessness is revealed" (2 Thessalonians 2:2-5).

The Revelation of John, finally, also contains passages that clearly indicate a longer process than we might expect on the basis of those texts quoted earlier, which emphasize the nearness of Christ's coming. A number of symbolic periods are to precede Jesus' return. An example is Revelation 11:3, in which two witnesses must prophesy for a specified period. Revelation 12:6 is another example; it mentions 1260 symbolic days during which God's church ("the woman") must hide to escape persecution. Much has been speculated about the true meaning of Revelation 6:9, especially about the souls under the altar. In whatever way this passage may best be explained, the cry "How long Sovereign Lord, holy and true, until you judge the inhabitants of the earth and avenge our blood?" (verse 10) is abundantly clear. The suffering and persecution lasts longer than they expected!

But enough about this. If the original New Testament authors did not feel the need to harmonize those elements of a *Naherwartung* with those pointing at a *Fernerwartung* (a near-expectation contrasted with a far-away expectation; the German language has concise words not found in other languages), why should this be our most urgent concern? Would we not do better to simply accept the New Testament tension between a "soon" and a "soon, but first..." and acknowledge that we, just as the Christians of the first century, may actually need such a tension in our religious experience?

## An unforeseen delay?

From the very beginning the so-called "delay" of the return of Christ posed a challenge to the Christian hope, says Richard Rice.

> "The evidence in the New Testament itself moved through several stages in its attitude to the Lord's return. Although they initially expected that this coming was very near, early Christians eventually concluded that he had been delayed."[6]

Yet, although "we see in the New Testament a development from immediacy to delay...the sense of immediacy never fully leaves the New Testament."[7]

A few texts are often quoted in connection with the delay of the second coming. The elements most commonly stressed are God's compassion and patience. The prophet Joel had already pointed to these characteristics of God when he said: "Return to the Lord your God, for he is gracious and compassionate, slow to anger and abounding in love" (Joel 2:13). God endures "with great patience the objects of his wrath" (Romans 9:22). He wants to give all people the opportunity to "return" and find salvation before it is too late; He wants "all people to be saved and to come to a knowledge of the truth" (1 Timothy 2:4). This same element is expressed by the apostle Peter: "The Lord is not slow in keeping his promise, as *some understand slowness*. Instead he is patient with you, not wanting anyone to perish, but everyone to come to repentance" (2 Peter 3:9). I have italicized a few words in the statement of Peter. These few words emphasize that our speaking about slowness and delay is based on our human perspective. We cannot see the complete picture. Said the prominent Dutch

---
[6] Richard Rice, *The Reign of God*, p. 380.
[7] Norman Gulley, *Christ is Coming: A Christ-centered Approach to Last-Day Events*, p. 540.

theologian G.C. Berkouwer (1903-1996): "The continuity of time is not evidence of a slack, indecisive God."[8] It may *appear* to us that this is the case, but this is only due to the limitations of our human understanding. Sakae Kubo agrees with this point of view: The delay arises out of a purely human reaction to human expectations. And he adds: "Emphasizing the nearness of the real coming in an almost time-setting way, will continue to develop a sense of delay."[9]

Ellen White stated on several occasions that the return of Christ could have taken place long ago if God's people had been more faithful in their witnessing. She writes in *The Desire of Ages:* "Had the church of Christ done her appointed work as the Lord ordained, the whole world would before this have been warned, and the Lord Jesus would have come to our earth in power and great glory."[10]

**When will Christ return?**

*Christ will come soon!* From the days of the apostles until today, time and time again Christians have confirmed their confidence in this promise. Ignatius, the bishop of Antioch (ca. 35-107), stated in his letter to the Ephesians, "These are the last times; let us feel shame, let us fear the patience of God, that it may not result in our condemnation (11:1)."[11] A second-century church leader called Barnabas, probably from Alexandria, wrote around the year 130, "The day is near when things will perish with the Evil one. The Lord is at hand, with his reward (21:3)."[12] The Church Father Cyprian (ca. 200-258) was

---

[8] G.C. Berkouwer, *The Return of Christ* (Grand Rapids, MI: William B. Eerdmans Publishing Company, 1972), p. 79.
[9] Sakae Kubo, *God Meets Man: A Theology of the Sabbath and Second Advent* (Nashville, TN: Southern Pub. Assn., 1978), pp. 100, 103.
[10] EGW, *The Desire of Ages*, pp. 633-634.
[11] Quoted from the translation by Eric J. Goodspeed, *The Apostolic Fathers: An American Translation* (London, UK: The Independent Press, 1950 ed.), p. 210.
[12] Quoted from Goodspeed, *The Apostolic Fathers*, p. 45.

sure that the end of the world was near. "The world has now grown old.... The whole world itself is already in the process of failing, and in its end.... The day of judgment is now drawing nigh."[13]

Centuries later John Wycliffe (ca. 1320-1384) emphasized the nearness of the second Advent. And for Martin Luther it was also clear that the end of the world could not be far away. In 1520 he wrote to the Germany nobility that he believed the judgment to be very near. "People try to penetrate into the secret of things to such an extent that today a young man of twenty knows more than formerly twenty scholars knew," he wrote in one of his sermons. In this he saw a direct fulfillment of Daniel's prophecy about the increase of knowledge in the time of the end (Daniel 12:4). In the year 1528 he was working on the translation of the book of Daniel into German. He hoped he would be able to finish this before the end came. On another occasion he said he doubted whether the world would still exist in 1548.[14]

John Wesley (1703-1791), the father of Methodism, likewise had no doubt about the impending end of this world. "We are very shortly to expect, one after the other, the calamities occasioned by the second beast." Following that statement he enumerated a number of other elements that link the Revelation of John to the coming of Christ. "How great are these things! And how short is time," he concluded.[15]

Truly, the Advent hope has been the hope of Christian believers throughout the Christian era. This was to be expected, given the central place of this hope in the entire New Testament. But it is astounding to see how many Christians in the past and up to the pres-

---

[13]Cyprian to Demetrianus, I.3, quoted from http://www.newadvent.org/fathers/050705.htm.
[14]Daniel Walter, "Martin Luther and the End of the World", *Ministry*, December, 1951; https://www.ministrymagazine.org/archive/1951/12/martin-luther-and-the-end-of-the-world.
[15]John Wesley, *Notes on the Bible*, Rev. 20:4, quoted from http://wesley.nnu.edu/john-wesley/john-wesleys-notes-on-the-bible/notes-on-the-revelation-of-jesus-christ/#Chapter+XX.

ent went beyond the information provided by the New Testament and were convinced they could actually pinpoint the exact time of Jesus' second coming, in spite of the straightforward declaration of the Lord Himself: "But about that day or hour no one knows, not even the angels in heaven, nor the Son, but only the Father" (Mark 13:32; cf. Matthew 24:36). It is certainly going against the obvious meaning of this text to suggest—as has repeatedly been done—that we may not be able to tell the *day* or *hour*, but that we can compute in what *year* Christ will come.

In spite of Christ's assertion that human beings cannot know the time of His return, through the ages believers have set dates. The followers of William Miller were not the first, nor the last, to do so. From time to time there have been advocates of a particular date for the second coming among Seventh-day Adventists. Thinking about the 120-year time period of Noah's warnings, some suggested that Adventists had been given that same time period, and that therefore the return of Christ, and thus of the end of the world, could be expected 120 years after 1844. Towards the end of the last century some Adventists proclaimed that the year 2000 might well signal the end of the world. The (very questionable) idea behind this was that the history of the earth had then been going on for 6,000 years and that now the 1,000 years of Revelation 20 would begin—in analogy of the six days of creation followed by the seventh-day Sabbath. It is strange how Adventist often base theories about the time of the end on a selective collection of Ellen G. White statements, while simply ignoring statements like this one:

> Many who have called themselves Adventists have been time setters. Time after time has been set for Christ to come, but

repeated failures have been the result. The definite time of our Lord's coming is declared to be beyond the ken of mortals. Even the angels who minister unto those who shall be heirs of salvation know not the day nor the hour. "But of that day and hour knoweth no man, no, not the angels of heaven, but My Father only."[16]

Since Christ's ascension there have been "signs of the times," like beacons so that we can be sure that the Advent *will* take place. Unfortunately, many readers of Matthew 24 and parallel chapters in the other synoptic Gospels get so excited when reading about the famines, wars, and earthquakes that they pay insufficient attention to the words of verse 8 that these disasters are just "the beginning of birth pains" and that when these things happen the end "will not come right away" (Luke 21:9).

**A sign of the end**

The only sign that seems to have an immediate link to the time of Christ's return is that of the preaching of the gospel. Note these words of Jesus: "This gospel of the kingdom will be preached in the whole world as a testimony to all nations, and then the end will come" (Matthew 24:14). But these words may not be as clear-cut as they seem at first sight. When can we be sure that the gospel is preached in the entire world? Is this when there is an Adventist missionary presence in each country of the world or in each part of every country? Or must every individual in this world have had the opportunity to hear and understand the gospel? And do we mean "gospel" in its general sense, or do we have the Adventist version of the gospel message in mind?

---
[16] EGW, *Testimonies for the Church*, vol. 4, p. 307.

Questions abound. Can we ever say that the work is finished? It is estimated that each day some 350,000 babies are born.[17] Must they not first grow up to an age when they can hear and understand the gospel? And, although we have communication technology on our side, it remains an enormous challenge to reach the population of our globe. Hundreds, if not thousands, of people groups must still be regarded as "unreached" with the good news of Jesus Christ, particularly in areas where Islam, Hinduism, or Buddhism are the dominant religions. Mission experts have calculated that around the year 1900 one-third of the world population could be considered Christian. A century later the percentage has hardly changed!

The supporters of Last Generation Theology have another approach: Christ will come when there is at long last a generation that perfectly reflects the character of Christ. We have already dealt with the topic of perfection and have seen how this cannot be a valid approach to determining when Christ will come. To me it sounds too much like the story of Levi, the Jewish rabbi who claimed that the Messiah would come when the Jews kept the Sabbath properly for even one day![18]

**Can we "hasten" Christ's coming?**

Many Adventist Christians are convinced that there is a definite relationship between the time of the second coming and our efforts to proclaim the gospel, with a special emphasis on the messages of the three angels of Revelation 14. The text that is most often quoted in support of this idea is found in 2 Peter 3:10-12. The KJV reads as follows:

---
[17] http://www.theworldcounts.com/stories/How-Many-Babies-Are-Born-Each-Day.
[18] Herold Weis, *A Day of Gladness: The Sabbath Among Jews and Christians in Antiquity* (Columbia, SC: The University of South Carolina Press, 2003), p. 11.

> But the day of the Lord will come as a thief in the night; in the which the heavens shall pass away with a great noise, and the elements shall melt with fervent heat, the earth also and the works that are therein shall be burned up. Seeing then that all these things shall be dissolved, what manner of persons ought ye to be in all holy conversation and godliness, looking for and hasting unto the coming of the day of God, wherein the heavens being on fire shall be dissolved, and the elements shall melt with fervent heat?

Verse 12 has the word "hasting" or "hastening," which seems to suggest that we can do our part in speeding up the day of the return of Christ. The New International Version (NIV), which I have mostly used in this book, actually uses that very word: we must "look forward to the day of God and speed its coming." In a popular Adventist paraphrase that wants to give the reader the "clear" meaning of the text, we find these words: "As we look forward to the day of Christ, let's do everything we can do to speed up its coming."[19] Eugene Peterson, the author of another (non-Adventist) paraphrase, thinks he has caught the true meaning of the text in these words: "Daily expect the Day of the Lord, eager for its arrival."[20] What rendering is closer to the original intent of the text?

Many English Bible translations have the word "hastening" or a synonym of that word in verse 12. However, experts of biblical Greek tell us that we must be careful in our interpretation of the Greek word *speudo,* which is often translated as "hastening" or "making come

---

[19]Jack J. Blanco, *The Clear Word: An Expanded Paraphrase of the Bible to Nurture Faith and Growth* (distributed by Review and Herald Publishing Association, 1994), p. 1391.
[20]Eugene H. Peterson, *The Message: The New Testament in Contemporary Language* (Colorado Springs, CO: NavPress Publishing Group, 1993), p. 498.

more quickly." It may be better to render it as "earnestly desiring" or something similar, as many translators insist.[21]

There may be a sense in which we can "hasten" the coming of the Lord through our missionary efforts. Ellen G. White appears to support this thought when she says: "By giving the gospel to the world it is in our power to hasten our Lord's return. We are not only to look for but to hasten the coming of the day of God."[22] And: "He has put it in our power, through co-operation with Him, to bring this scene of misery to an end."[23]

But there can only be a "speeding up" or "hastening" from a human perspective. God has always known when the end of the world will come and when His Son will return to deliver His people. I believe Norman Gulley hits the nail on its head when he states: "God's foreknowledge took into consideration all of human hastening and delaying and simply fed all the data in his computer to arrive at the appropriate date."[24] The following short paragraph is also worth quoting:

> The fact that God knows the end from the beginning should not suggest determinism or a kind of fatalism. God does not predestinate, or predetermine, human destiny against human volition. Nor does He arbitrarily set the return date. On the other hand humans cannot—in the ultimate sense—hasten or delay that date either—at least in the absolute sense. Or else Christ may never come.[25]

---
[21]Sakae Kubo, *God Meets Man*, p. 101.
[22]EGW, *The Desire of Ages*, p. 633.
[23]EGW, *Education*, p. 264.
[24]Norman Gulley, *Christ is Coming*, p. 542.
[25]*Ibid.*

Gulley concludes his remarks on the topic of the hastening of Christ's coming with these significant words: "If humans could really hasten the Advent by themselves, Christians would face the greatest salvation-by-works emphasis ever—in spite of the gospel."[26] Kubo puts this point even more poignantly: "It is well to keep this in mind that we do not blasphemously think that we can somehow by our own merely human efforts bring Christ down."[27]

**Reckoning *with*, rather than reckoning**

The same passage that (in some Bible versions) refers to the "hastening" of the Lord's coming emphasizes another aspect of the second coming. The day of the Lord will come "as a thief in the night" (2 Peter 3:10, KJV). This reminds us of the description Jesus gave of the suddenness of His coming: "On that night two people will be in one bed; one will be taken and the other left. Two women will be grinding grain together; one will be taken and the other left" (Luke 17:34-35).

As we have seen, other passages in the Bible tell us that a series of different events must take place before the end will come. The charts of future events that are so popular with many Adventists present us with a detailed scenario of end-time events that precede the second coming. They seem to contradict the thief-in-the-night picture and to tell us that we should not be taken by surprise, for there is really no suddenness about Christ's return.

What do we do with this apparent paradox? I suggest that we leave this for what it is. Our understanding of what will exactly transpire before we see Christ "on the clouds of heaven" is, and will remain, very limited. Our experience of time is very human and the apostle Peter reminds us of the fact that God's sense of time is quite

---
[26]Ibid.
[27]Sakae Kubo, *God Meets Man*, p. 101.

different. "With the Lord a day is like a thousand years, and a thousand years are like a day" (2 Peter 3:8). Does this mean that any time element mentioned in the Bible has absolutely no meaning for us? No, for after all, God wants to communicate with us and He does so in language and images that we can relate to. But, at the same time, Peter's words remind us that, when all is said and done, God's timing cannot be one-on-one compared to our sense of the passing of time.

However, of one thing, the apostle Peter stresses, we may be totally sure: "The Lord is not slow in keeping his promise" (2 Peter 3:9). The Dutch theologian Berkouwer summarizes what, in view of God's promise, our attitude should be: "The believer is called to an attitude that does not *reckon*, but that constantly *reckons with* the coming of the Lord."[28] Samuel Bacchiocchi agrees: The purpose of this tension between texts that emphasize the nearness and the remoteness of the second coming is "to discourage speculation and calculation of the date and to encourage constant preparation."[29]

As Christian believers who long for the return of their Lord, we will watch for the signs all along the way. We want to be ready, at any time, for we do not know when Jesus comes. We need to "keep watch, because [we] do not know the day or the hour" (Matthew 25:13), and we must realize that our last day may be today or tomorrow. The final developments in our world may be quick and may well surprise us. But considering the inevitable limitations in our understanding of biblical prophecy, things may turn out in ways that differ substantially from the pattern we have inherited in our Adventist tradition.

Years ago theologian and pastor John Brunt wrote a little book about the second coming that continues to be a very worthwhile read.

---

[28] G.C. Berkouwer, *The Return of Christ*, p. 84.
[29] Samuele Bacchiocchi, *The Advent Hope and Human Hopelessness* (Berrien Springs, MI: Biblical Perspectives, 1986), p. 109.

After referring to the New Testament comparison of Christ's second coming with a wedding feast, he wonders: "If the Second Coming is something like a wedding, why don't we who believe in it share more of the joy and eager anticipation of a bride?" Brunt thinks there are three reasons. In the first place, he says, we often seem to be unsure about the One who is to come. Can we trust Him? His justice seems to be so severe. There seems to be a dark shadow hanging over the end of history and over the painful transition to the new world that has been promised. Secondly, we are often unsure of ourselves. Are we prepared to the extent that we should be? Are we good enough to endure the end of time, and will we be found worthy to enter His kingdom? Thirdly, Brunt tells us, unfortunately we too often "focus our attention on the events that occur before the Second Coming instead of on the One who comes and the new kingdom He has prepared for us. It is true that things on this earth will get worse before the Second Coming, but we have the promise that God will be with us. Besides, all this is nothing in comparison with the joy of being with God in our new home."[30]

**Our living hope**

The essence our Christian experience is the living hope in which we may "greatly rejoice" (1 Peter 1:4-6). According to Richard Rice there are several things this hope involves and several things it does not. It does not, for instance, require us to know exactly when Christ will come. Rice mentions four essential qualities of that hope:

1. It includes the *certainty* that Christ will return. Without that certainty there is no hope but only despair.
2. It includes *wanting* Christ to come. "We live without hope if we

---
[30]John Brunt, *Now & Not Yet* (Hagerstown, MD: Review and Herald Pub. Assn., 1987), pp. 86-88.

live entirely for the present." Living for Christ's return must be "the ultimate object of life."

3. It involves *watchfulness*, knowing that Christ may come at any time. "We lose hope when we relegate the return of Christ to the remote and irrelevant future," without any immediate significance for our life today.
4. It includes preparation and means "fulfilling our present responsibilities with enthusiasm and dependability."[31]

Before closing this chapter I want to stress again what I emphasized in other chapters. We should be utterly grateful for all the things we know about the end of time and about the glorious return of our Lord. But we must constantly recognize, in all humility, that there are many aspects we cannot be sure about and must leave in the hands of our heavenly Father. Whether we may speak of a "delay" in Christ's coming and can, from a human perspective, actually "hasten" the second coming may remain a matter of debate, but we can all rejoice in the fact that we may eagerly long for the great day!

---

[31] Richard Rice, *The Reign of God*, pp. 361-362.

# Chapter 9

# In All Humility

A dictionary definition of humility is "The quality or condition of being humble." And the word "humble" is further defined as "marked by meekness or modesty in behavior, attitude and spirit."[1] Humility is a virtue for all people. But Christians are called to be humble in a very special sense. In the well-known text about Christ's incarnation, we are told that Christ "humbled himself" in an ultimate manner, and that we should "have the same mindset as Christ Jesus" (Philippians 2:5-8). As the eventual reward for practicing humility, God's servants "will be exalted" (Matthew 23:12).

Humility is not a form of self-negation. It has nothing to do with low self-esteem or servile self-loathing.[2] It describes an attitude of knowing our place and of avoiding all boasting about our imagined or real capabilities. In a religious sense it refers to knowing our status before God. We may rejoice in the fact that we have been created in the image of God (Genesis 1:26), that He has made us only "a little lower than the angels" (Psalm 8:5), and that He crowned us "with glory and honor" (Hebrews 2:7). However, this does not make us equals

---
[1] *The American Heritage Dictionary*, third edition (Boston: Houghton Mifflin Company, 1992), pp. 881-880.
[2] Helen Oppenheimer, "Humility," in John Macquarrie and James Childress, *A New Dictionary of Christian Ethics* (London, UK: SMC Press, 1986 ed.), p. 284.

with our Creator. We are finite, limited, earthly beings who stand in awe before our infinite, omniscient heavenly Father.

All our knowing is always "in part" (1 Corinthians 13:9). When it comes to divine truth, "we see only a reflection as in a mirror" and must wait till we see the Lord face to face. We must echo the words of Paul: "Now I know in part; then I shall know fully" (1 Corinthians 13:12).

**Knowing in part**

When I study Adventist history and also try to take the pulse of contemporary Adventism, I cannot escape the feeling that a sense of pride that "we have the truth" has often hampered our humility, and that in outlining the last-day events we have frequently given the impression that we know it all, rather than in all modesty and humility acknowledging that we only know in part. This is what I have tried to emphasize in this book about Last Generation Theology and why I have entitled it *In All Humility*.

I hope that those who have read this book in its entirety will have come to the same conclusion as I have when studying this matter: The Bible is crystal clear about the reality of our Advent hope and about the trustworthiness of Jesus' parting promise, "I will come again." The Bible gives us sufficient information about what to expect and how to prepare for that glorious event. It teaches all we need to know to make an informed choice—for or against God. However, at the same time we must recognize that the Bible is not as clear on some aspects of eschatology as many think, and that numerous questions will remain unanswered as long as we are in this world. In addition, we must also recognize that Ellen White's comments are not always totally clear and that at times they may even seem somewhat inconsistent. For some Adventists this presents a major problem. I believe, however, that this should not worry us unduly, as long as we have a proper understanding of her role as a "lesser light" that points to the "greater light" of the Bible. And, when everything is said and done, we must go to the Bible for the final answer.

**Recognizing the problems in Last Generation Theology**

As we approach the end of this book, some readers may feel disappointed. They may have discovered that I have not provided all the answers they hoped to get. Some may feel that I should have treated particular aspects in more depth, or they may believe this book has other deficiencies. I am sure this book is not perfect and that much more could have been said on various issues. My primary intention in writing this book has been to convince as many of my fellow Adventists as possible that Last Generation Theology has some very serious flaws and even presents some significant dangers. I hope and pray that this book will cause many to think these subjects through in a new way and with an open mind.

Let me briefly summarize the problems that I see in Last Generation Theology:
- an inadequate doctrine of sin,
- a serious misunderstanding of the human nature of Christ,
- an inadequate, one-sided view of perfection,
- the very real danger of fostering an attitude of legalism,
- a wrong perception of the so-called "shaking,"
- a far too narrow view of the concept of the remnant,
- a questionable view about the close of probation and of living without a Mediator,
- a one-sided view of the possibility of delaying and hastening the coming of the Lord.

**What we do know for certain**

There will, undoubtedly, remain many questions, and we may never find satisfying answers to all of them. However, we are not left with only question marks. There are a number of crucial things we can be absolutely certain about:

- We are sinful and will remain sinful as long as we are in this world.
- Christ has come to our world, and He became fully human. He became truly one of us and could therefore identify with us. How He could be fully God and fully man at the same time, and in what sense He became fully man, is beyond our finite human understanding. He is our Savior—that is all we need to know.
- The goal of sinless perfection is beyond our reach. However, we have the promise that when Christ comes we will be resurrected as, or changed into, perfect beings.
- Christ will come "soon," but we will never be able to calculate the date of His return. From our human perspective it may seem that He has delayed His coming, but God has determined the time of the return of His Son and His promise is as sure as ever.
- The situation in our world will heat up. God's people will have to live through difficult times, but God will never leave us alone in a situation in which we have to rely on our own strength. He will care for us until the very end, in whatever circumstances we may find ourselves.
- There will always be a people of God—a remnant. We do not need to know who exactly will constitute this remnant and how large it will be. And God may very well surprise us.

- We are called to make preparations and be ready for the great day of Christ's coming. As long as time lasts, we must do what we can for this world and must continue to invite people to live as disciples of Christ in this world and prepare for the next.

That much we know and that is all we need to know. Let us be humble enough to realize our limitations and be content with our partial, incomplete understanding that we have been granted.

As I call upon my readers to engage in this exercise of humility, I stand ready to acknowledge my own limitations in writing this book. I have criticized the Last Generation Theology supporters for their selectivity in their Bible reading and, in particular, in their use of Ellen White statements. I must, however, admit that I also read selectively and cannot fully escape from all my prejudices. We all read through our own spectacles. Nevertheless, I have done my best to give as honest an appraisal of Last Generation Theology as I can. And in spite of all the imperfections this book no doubt manifests, I sincerely hope it will help many to see, and avoid, the pitfalls of Last Generation Theology.

My conclusion is that Last Generation Theology is defective in many of the things it teaches. It claims to know too many things that it cannot really know. It draws conclusions that cannot be supported by biblical evidence. It confuses many people with its view of a perfect final generation and threatens to draw them into a kind of legalism that obscures the immeasurable grace of Christ.

Let us in all humility commit ourselves to Christ and totally rely on Him for our salvation. Let us worship Him as His loyal disciples, aware of all our shortcomings, but trusting that He will continue to be with us—if we stay on His side—and that in the end He will pull us through.

# Bibliography

Adams, Roy. *The Nature of Christ: Help for a Church Divided Over Perfection.* Hagerstown, MD: Review and Herald Pub. Assn., 1994.

Adams, Roy. *The Sanctuary: Understanding the Heart of Adventist Theology.* Hagerstown, MD: Review and Herald Pub. Assn., 1993.

Andreasen, M.L. *The Sanctuary Service.* Washington, DC: Review and Herald Pub. Assn., 1947, second edition.

Bacchiocchi, Samuele. *The Advent Hope and Human Hopelessness.* Berrien Springs, MI: Biblical Perspectives, 1986.

Ball, Bryan W., and Johnsson, William G., eds. *The Essential Jesus: The Man, the Message, the Mission.* Boise, ID: Pacific Press Pub. Assn., 2002.

Barna, Jan. *Adventism and Biblical Perfection: The Diverse Roots of Perfectionist Thinking in Adventism and the Need for Biblical Definition of Perfection* (paper presented during the Bible Symposium on Perfectionism: Adventism and Biblical Perfection, South England Conference, Feb. 5, 2013).

Berkouwer, G.C. *The Return of Christ.* Grand Rapids, MI: William B. Eerdmans Publishing Company, 1972.

Berkouwer, G.C. *Studies in Dogmatics: Faith and Sanctification.* Grand Rapids, MI: William. B. Eerdmans Publishing Company, 1952.

Berkouwer, G.C. *Studies in Dogmatics: The Person of Christ.* Grand Rapids, MI: William. B. Eerdmans Publishing Company, 1954.

Blanco, Jack J. *The Clear Word: An Expanded Paraphrase of the Bible to Nurture Faith and Growth* (distributed by Review and Herald Publishing Association, 1994).

Blazen, Ivan. "Salvation," in *Handbook of Seventh-day Adventist Theology.* Hagerstown, MD: Review & Herald Pub. Association, 2000.

Blowers, Paul M. "Perfectionism," in *New Westminster Dictionary of*

*Church History*. Louisville, KY: Westminster John Knox Press, 2008.

Brown, Colin Brown, ed. *The New International Dictionary of New Testament Theology*. Exeter, GB: The Paternoster Press, 1976.

Bruinsma, Reinder. *The Body of Christ: A Biblical Understanding of the Church*. Hagerstown, MD: Review and Herald Pub. Assn., 2009.

Bruinsma, Reinder. *Facing Doubt: A Book for Adventist Believers 'on the Margins.'* London, UK: Flankó Press, 2016.

Bruinsma, Reinder. *Faith, Step by Step: Finding God and Yourself.* Grantham, UK: Stanborough Press, 2006.

Bruinsma, Reinder. *Keywords of the Christian Faith*. Hagerstown, MD: Review and Herald Pub. Assn., 2008.

Bruinsma, Reinder. *Van Komst naar Wederkomst*. Huis ter Heide/Brussel: Uitgeverij Veritas, 1997.

Brunt, John. *Now & Not Yet*. Hagerstown, MD: Review and Herald Pub. Assn., 1987.

Chaij Fernando. *Preparing for the Final Crisis*. Nampa, ID: Pacific Press Pub. Assn., 1998.

Coon, Roger W. "Shaking," in Denis Fortin and Jerry Moon, eds., *The Ellen G. White Encyclopedia*. Hagerstown, MD: Review and Herald Pub. Assn., 2014,

Cyprian to Demetrianus, I.3, quoted from http://www.newadvent.org/fathers/050705.htm.

Dederen, Raoul. ed. *Commentary Reference Series*. Hagerstown: Review and Herald Pub. Assn., 2000.

Dederen, Raoul, ed. *Handbook of Seventh-day Adventist Theology*. Hagerstown, MD: Review and Herald Pub. Assn., 2000.

Douglas, Herbert E., Heppenstall, Edward, LaRondelle, Hans K., and Maxwell, C. Mervyn. *Perfection: The Impossible Possibility*. Nashville, TN: Southern Pub. Assn., 1975.

Edwards, Calvin W. and Land, Gary. *Seeker after Light: A.F. Ballenger, Adventism, and American Christianity*. Berrien Springs, MI: Andrews University Press, 2000.

Flew, R. Newton. *The Idea of Perfection in Christian Theology*. Eugene, OR: Wipf and Stock, 2005 edition.

Fortin, Denis. "Ellen White on the Human Nature of Christ," https://www.andrews.edu/~fortind/EGWNatureofChrist.htm.

Goldstein, Clifford. *1844 Made Simple*. Nampa, ID: Pacific Press Pub. Assn., 1998.

Goodspeed, Eric J. *The Apostolic Fathers: An American Translation*. London, UK: The Independent Press, 1950.

Gulley, Norman. *Christ is Coming: A Christ-centered Approach to Last-Day Events*. Hagerstown, MD: Review and Herald Pub. Association, 1998.

Horton, Michael. *The Christian Faith: A Systematic Theology for Pilgrims on the Way*. Grand Rapids, MI: Zondervan, 2011.

http://advindicate.com/articles/2017/5/21/five-popular-myths-about-last-generation-theology.

http://documents.adventistarchives.org/Periodicals/GCSessionBulletins/GCB1895-01-13ex.pdf.

http://www.adventistreview.org/assets/public/news/2014-12/humanatureChristfallen.pdf.

http://www.ccel.org/ccel/wesley/perfection.ii.vi.html.

www.gotquestions.org/Keswick-movement.html.

http://www.theworldcounts.com/stories/How-Many-Babies-Are-Born-Each-Day.

https://dictionary.cambridge.org/dictionary/english/paradox.

https://en.wikipedia.org/wiki/Herbert E. Douglass.

https://en.wikipedia.org/wiki/Robert_Brinsmead.

https://m.egwwritings.org/en/book/1623.2000136#153.

https://text.egwwritings.org/publication.php?pubtype=Book&bookCode=1888&pagenumber=560.

https://www.facebook.com/PastorTedWilson/posts/924770757578817:0.

Jacobs, A. J. *The Year of Living Biblically: One Man's Humble Quest to Follow the Bible as Literally as Possible.* New York: Simon and Schuster, 2007.

Kelley, J.N.D. *Early Christian Creeds.* London: Longmans, Green and Co., Ltd, 1967.

Knight, George R. *From 1888 to Apostasy: The Case of A.T. Jones.* Hagerstown: MD: Review and Herald Pub. Assn., 1987.

Knight, George R. *Matthew: The Gospel of the Kingdom.* Nampa, ID: Pacific Press Pub. Assn., 1994).

Knight, George R. *A Search for Identity: The Development of Seventh-day Adventist Beliefs.* Hagerstown, MD: Review and Herald Pub. Assn., 2000.

Knight, George R. *Sin and Salvation: God's Work for and in Us.* Hagerstown, MD: Review and Herald Pub. Assn., 2008.

Knight, George R. *A User-Friendly Guide to the 1888 Message.* Hagerstown, MD: Review and Herald Pub. Assn., 1998.

Kubo, Sakae. *God Meets Man: A Theology of the Sabbath and Second Advent.* Nashville, TN: Southern Pub. Assn., 1978.

LaRondelle, H.K. *Perfection and Perfectionism: A Dogmatic-Ethical Study of Biblical Perfection and Phenomenal Perfectionism.* Kampen, the Netherlands: J.H. Kok NV, 1971.

Larson, Ralph. *The Word Was Made Flesh: One Hundred Years of Seventh-day Adventist Christology 1852-1952.* Fort Oglethorpe, GA:

TEACH Services, Inc., 1986.

Lewis, C. S. *Mere Christianity*. New York: HarperCollins Publishers, 1980 edition.

Macquarrie, John and Childress, James. *A New Dictionary of Christian Ethics*. London, UK: SMC Press, 1986.

McGrath, Alister. *Christelijke Theologie: Een Introductie*. Kampen: Uitgeverij Kok, 1997.

McMahon, David P. *Ellet Joseph Waggoner: The Myth and the Man*. Fallbrook, CA: Verdict Publications, 1979.

Moore, Marvin. *The Case for the Investigative Judgment: Its Biblical Foundation*. Nampa, ID: Pacific Press Pub. Assn., 2010.

Moore, Marvin. *The Crisis of the End Time*. Boise, ID: Pacific Press Pub. Assn., 1992.

Moore, Marvin. *How to Think About the End Time*. Nampa, ID: Pacific Press Pub. Assn., 2001.

Moore, Marvin. *The Refiner's Fire*. Nampa, ID: The Pacific Press Pub. Assn., 2014.

Nichol, Francis, ed. *The Seventh-day Adventist Bible Commentary*. Washington, DC: Review and Herald Pub. Assn., 1956.

Paulien, Jon. *What the Bible Says About the End-Time*. Hagerstown, MD: Review and Herald Pub. Assn., 1994.

Paxton, Geoffrey J. *The Shaking of Adventism*. Grand Rapids, MI: Baker Book House, 1978.

Peterson, Eugene H. *The Message: The New Testament in Contemporary Language*. Colorado Springs, CO: NavPress Publishing Group, 1993.

Poirier, Tim. "Sources Clarify Ellen White's Christology." *Ministry*, Dec. 1989.

Rice, Richard. *The Reign of God: An Introduction to Christian Theology from a Seventh-day Adventist Perspective.* Berrien Springs, MI: Andrews University Press, 1997, second edition.

Rice, Richard. "Sanctification and Perfection: Another Look." *Ministry*, June 1984.

Rodriguez, Manuel, "The Remnant and the Adventist Church," www.adventistbiblicalresearch.org/sites/default/files/pdf/remnantSDAchurch_0.pdf.

Schwarz, Richard W. and Greenleaf, Floyd. *Light Bearers: A History of the Seventh-day Adventist Church.* Nampa, ID: Pacific Press Pub. Assn., 1995.

*Seventh-day Adventist Encyclopedia.* Hagerstown, MD: Review and Herald Pub. Assn., 1996.

*Seventh-day Adventists Answer Questions on Doctrine*, annotated edition, with historical and theological introduction by George R. Knight. Berrien Springs, MI: Andrews University Press, 2003.

*Seventh-day Adventists Believe.* Silver Spring, MD: Ministerial Association, General Conference of Seventh-day Adventists, 2005, second edition.

Steinweg, Virgina. *Without Fear or Favor.* Washington, DC: Review and Herald Pub. Assn., 1979.

Tarling, Lowell. *The Edges of Seventh-day Adventism.* Barragga Bay, Australia: Galilee Publishing, 1981.

*The American Heritage Dictionary,* third edition. Boston: Houghton Mifflin Company, 1992.

Van der Kooi, Cornelis and van den Brink, Gijsbert. *Christian Dogmatics: An Introduction.* Grand Rapids, MI: William B. Eerdmans Publishing Company, 2017.

Vick, Edward. *Let Me Assure You: Of Grace, of Faith, of Forgiveness, of Freedom, of Fellowship, of Hope.* Mountain View, CA: Pacific Press

Pub. Assn., 1968.

Waggoner, E.J. "God Manifest in the Flesh." *Signs of the Times*, Jan. 21, 1889.

Wallenkampf, Arnold V. and Lesher, W. Richard. *The Sanctuary and the Atonement: Biblical, Historical and Theological Studies*. General Conf. of SDA, Biblical Research Institute, 1981.

Walter, Daniel. "Martin Luther and the End of the World", *Ministry*, December, 1951.

Webster, Eric C. *Crosscurrents in Adventist Christology*. Berrien Springs, MI: Andrews University Press, 1992.

Weis, Herold. *A Day of Gladness: The Sabbath Among Jews and Christians in Antiquity*. Columbia, SC: The University of South Carolina Press, 2003.

Wesley, John. *Notes on the Bible*, Rev. 20:4, quoted from http://wesley.nnu.edu/john-wesley/john-wesleys-notes-on-the-bible/notes-on-the-revelation-of-jesus-christ/#Chapter+XX.

Wesley, John. *A Plain Account of Christian Perfection*. London: Epsworth, 1952.

Whidden, Woodrow. *Ellen White on the Humanity of Christ*. Hagerstown, MD; Review and Herald Pub. Assn., 1997.

Whidden, Woodrow. *From the Physician of Good News to the Agent of Division*. Hagerstown, MD: Review and Herald Pub. Assn., 2008.

Whidden, Woodrow W. *The Soteriology of Ellen G White: The Persistent Path to Perfection, 1836-1902*. Madison, NJ: Drew University, 1989.

White, Ellen G. "Behold What Manner of Love." *The Review and Herald*, Sept. 27, 1906.

White, Ellen G. "Child Life of Jesus." *The Signs of the Times*, July 30, 1896.

White, Ellen G. "Christ's Triumph in Our Behalf." *The Signs of the Times*, August 4, 1887.

White, Ellen G. "Conquer Through the Conqueror." *Review and Herald*, Feb. 5, 1895.

White, Ellen G. "The First Advent of Christ." *The Review and Herald*, Dec. 24, 1872.

White, Ellen G. "The Importance of Obedience." *The Review and Herald*, Dec. 15, 1896.

White, Ellen G. "Lessons from the Second Chapter of Philippians." *The Review and Herald*, June 15, 1905.

White, Ellen G. "Meetings in Chicago." *The Review and Herald*, Feb. 10, 1885.

White, Ellen G. "No Excuse for Relaxing Self-discipline." *The Review and Herald*, Oct. 1, 1889.

White, Ellen G. "Recount God's Dealings." *The Review and Herald*, March 19, 1895.

White, Ellen G. "Satan's Rebellion." *The Signs of the Times*, July 23, 1902.

White, Ellen G. "Search the Scriptures." *The Youth's Instructor*, Oct. 13, 1898.

White, Ellen G. "The Signal of Advance." *The Review and Herald*, Jan. 20, 1903.

White, Ellen G. "Thoughts on the First Epistle of John." *The Signs of the Times*, May 23, 1895.

White, Ellen G. "The Whole Duty of Man." *The Signs of the Times*, May 16, 1895.

White, Ellen G. *Christ's Object Lessons*. Washington, D.C.: Review and Herald Publishing Association, 1941.

White, Ellen G. *Christian Service*. Hagerstown, MD: Review and Herald Publishing Association, 1947.

White, Ellen G. *The Desire of Ages*. Mountain View, CA: Pacific Press Publishing Association, 1940.

White, Ellen G. *Early Writings*. Washington, D.C.: Review and Herald Publishing Association, 1945.

White, Ellen G. *Education*. 1903. Mountain View, CA: Pacific Press Publishing Association, 1952.

White, Ellen G. *The Great Controversy*. Mountain View, CA: Pacific Press Publishing Association, 1911.

White, Ellen G. *In Heavenly Places*. Washington, D.C.: Review and Herald Publishing Association, 1967.

White, Ellen G. *Last Day Events*. Boise, ID: Pacific Press Publishing Association, 1992.

White, Ellen G. *Letter 15* (June 27, 1892).

White, Ellen G. *Letter 46* (April 22, 1887).

White, Ellen G. *Letter 48* (1876).

White, Ellen G. *Manuscript 1*, 1857.

White, Ellen G. *Manuscript 125*, 1907.

White, Ellen G. *Manuscript Releases, vol. 16*. Silver Spring, MD: Ellen G. White Estate, 1981, 1987, 1990, 1993.

White, Ellen G. *Manuscript Releases, vol. 21*. Silver Spring, MD: Ellen G. White Estate, 1981, 1987, 1990, 1993.

White, Ellen G. *Manuscript Releases, vol. 7*. Silver Spring, MD: Ellen G. White Estate, 1981, 1987, 1990, 1993.

White, Ellen G. *MS 93*, 1893.

White, Ellen G. *MS 94*, June 30, 1893.

White, Ellen G. *Our High Calling*. Washington, D.C.: Review and Herald Publishing Association, 1961.

White, Ellen G. *Prophets and Kings*. Mountain View, CA: Pacific Press

Publishing Association, 1943.

White, Ellen G. *Selected Messages, vol. 1*. Washington, D.C.: Review and Herald Publishing Association, 1958, 1980.

White, Ellen G. *Selected Messages, vol. 3*. Washington, D.C.: Review and Herald Publishing Association, 1958, 1980.

White, Ellen G. *Sons and Daughters of God*. Washington, D.C.: Review and Herald Publishing Association, 1955.

White, Ellen G. *The Spirit of Prophecy, vol. 3*. Battle Creek, MI: Seventh-day Adventist Publishing Association, 1969.

White, Ellen G. *Spiritual Gifts, vol. 4a*. Battle Creek, MI: Seventh-day Adventist Publishing Association, 1945

White, Ellen G. *Steps to Christ*. Mountain View, CA: Pacific Press, 1956.

White, Ellen G. *Testimonies for the Church, vol. 1*. Mountain View, CA: Pacific Press Publishing Association, 1948.

White, Ellen G. *Testimonies for the Church, vol. 2*. Mountain View, CA: Pacific Press Publishing Association, 1948.

White, Ellen G. *Testimonies for the Church, vol. 3*. Mountain View, CA: Pacific Press Publishing Association, 1948.

White, Ellen G. *Testimonies for the Church, vol. 4*. Mountain View, CA: Pacific Press Publishing Association, 1948.

White, Ellen G. *Testimonies for the Church, vol. 5*. Mountain View, CA: Pacific Press Publishing Association, 1948.

White, Ellen G. *Testimonies for the Church, vol. 6*. Mountain View, CA: Pacific Press Publishing Association, 1948.

Yancey, Philip. *What's So Amazing About Grace?* Grand Rapids, MI: Zondervan Publishing House, 1997.

Printed in Great Britain
by Amazon